All Our Children

All Our Children

The Church's Call to Address Education Inequity

edited by **Lallie B. Lloyd**
foreword by **Gay Clark Jennings**

Church Publishing
NEW YORK

Unless otherwise noted, the Scripture quotations contained herein are from the New Revised Standard Version Bible, copyright © 1989 by the Division of Christian Education of the National Council of Churches of Christ in the U.S.A. Used by permission. All rights reserved.

Scripture quotations marked (ESV) are from the ESV® Bible (The Holy Bible, English Standard Version®), copyright © 2001 by Crossway, a publishing ministry of Good News Publishers. Used by permission. All rights reserved

Church Publishing
19 East 34th Street
New York, NY 10016
www.churchpublishing.org

Cover design by Jennifer Kopec, 2Pug Design
Typeset by PerfecType, Nashville, Tennessee

Library of Congress Cataloging-in-Publication Data

A record of this book is available from the Library of Congress.

ISBN-13: 978-0-8192-3347-9 (pbk.)
ISBN-13: 978-0-8192-3348-6 (ebook)

Printed in the United States of America

To all our grandchildren

Contents

Acknowledgments

I am grateful to the authors whose stories are the heart and soul of this book; to the members of All Our Children's leadership team over the years, including Yamily Bass-Choate, Ben Campbell, Don Cowles, Bill Franklin, Meg McDermott, Suellyn Scull, Anne Tuohy, and Vicki Zust; and to my colleague Mary-Liz Murray, whose skill and professionalism are matched by her good humor and open heart.

This network, this movement, this dream would not be manifest in the world as it is today without the early, abiding, and generous support of Trinity Wall Street.

Foreword

In May 2016, just after the sixty-second anniversary of the Supreme Court's decision in *Brown vs. Board of Education*, I traveled to Buffalo, New York, at the kind invitation of my friends Dean Will Mebane and Bishop Bill Franklin to attend an All Our Children forum. The timing was auspicious for a gathering of Episcopalians concerned with equity in public education. *Brown vs. Board*, which struck down state laws establishing racially segregated schools, was argued before the Court for the plaintiffs by Thurgood Marshall, an Episcopalian and deputy to the 1964 General Convention. We celebrate the Feast of Thurgood Marshall on May 17 in honor of his fight for justice in our schools and our society.

But, as I said in Buffalo, we need to do more than just honor the struggle of those who went before us. *Brown vs. Board* changed laws, but in the six decades since that landmark decision, the gains we achieved toward a system of public education that treated all students fairly, regardless of their race, have largely disappeared. *The Atlantic* recently reported that an analysis of federal data reveals that "in virtually every major U.S. metropolitan area students of color are much more likely than whites to attend public schools shaped by high concentrations of poverty."[1]

As community members, we know that the toxic mix of segregation and poverty found in far too many of our public schools is the product of failed social policies that cost taxpayers billions of dollars that flow through the school-to-prison pipeline. As Christians, we know that we are not respecting the dignity of every human being when children attend deteriorating

---

1. http://www.theatlantic.com/education/archive/2016/03/separate-still-unequal/471720/

public schools that cannot possibly help them reach their potential. And as Episcopalians, we know what we need to do.

Luckily, Lallie Lloyd and the passionate advocates of All Our Children have picked up the mantle of our brother Thurgood Marshall and can show us the way. Their work is buttressed by Resolution B005 of the 2015 General Convention of the Episcopal Church, which endorses church-school partnerships. The resolution's explanation details the staggering human and financial cost of educational disparity in the United States and says, "The church speaks a word of truth into this bleakness—holding a mirror to this scandal with unvarnished clarity. The church also brings a message of hope . . ."

In these pages, you will read about Episcopalians who are bringing messages of hope and holding up mirrors. At our very best, we Episcopalians are good at doing both. We can show up to tutor children, and we can speak at school board meetings where funds for reading teachers are on the table. We can collect school supplies and backpacks for children who need them, and we can meet with our state legislators and insist that the state budget fund education in more equitable ways. We can make sure kids get lunch during the summer when they might go hungry, and we can vote for candidates who support child nutrition programs. We can welcome immigrant and refugee families to our local schools, and we can refuse to countenance bigoted, hate-filled speech about immigrants with either our silence or our votes.

We can do charity, and we can do justice. We Episcopalians understand that acts of mercy and loving kindness matter most when they go hand in hand with advocacy that seeks to eliminate the root causes of poverty, inequality, injustice, and violence. Church-school partnerships give us the chance to do both, and I hope that the stories you are about to read will inspire you to join the All Our Children movement.

The Reverend Gay Clark Jennings
President, House of Deputies of the Episcopal Church
December 2016

Introduction

Like other religions and denominations, the Episcopal Church has for many years and in many ways affirmed the importance of quality public education for all children as a justice issue, a moral issue, and a community issue. Since 1985, Episcopalians have passed resolutions at eight General Conventions and participated in ecumenical and interfaith collaborations resulting in documents such as the National Council of Churches of Christ in the U.S.A.'s "The Church and Children: Vision and Goals for the 21st Century" policy statement in 2012.[1]

However, the quality of US public education has deteriorated over these same decades.

More than twenty years after he was fired for teaching a Langston Hughes poem to black fourth graders in Boston, Jonathan Kozol spent two years documenting the inequities between rich and poor students in cities like Detroit, New York, San Antonio, and Chicago. He documented in vivid heart-wrenching prose the inequalities between rich and poor children at school. In 1991 Kozol called his landmark book *Savage Inequalities*, and we are required to acknowledge now that our inequalities have become even more savage.

The Church's statements, agreements, and resolutions have had little impact, which should not surprise us. Resolutions are not enough.

---

1. See http://nationalcouncilofchurches.us/common-witness/2012/children.php (accessed October 12, 2016).

The Episcopal Public Policy Network (EPPN),[2] which implements national policy positions taken by General Convention can be of limited help here, in part because none of the Episcopal Church's education resolutions directs a specific federal action, and in part because the federal role in education is dwarfed by the state and local roles. Only 8.3 percent[3] of the total funding for K-12 education comes from Washington, so while the US Department of Education has powerful regulatory and programmatic influence—and this is where the EPPN can make a difference—the US Constitution is unequivocal that public education is a state responsibility: it is a matter for our states, cities, and towns. To make a difference in public education, the church needs to be involved locally, regionally, and statewide.

About This Book

Instead of approaching the question of the church's role in addressing our national education crisis as an abstraction ("What *should* the church do?"), we have instead gathered concrete examples of what the church is actually doing. When we ask about "the church's" role in addressing education inequity, we acknowledge that the church is both an institution and a movement. This bipolar reality explains why some passages in this book describe the church's role as either bottom-up or top-down. Resolutions, programs, and large initiatives proposed by church conventions bookend what local people in local contexts are doing in response to their particular calls from the Holy Spirit to act in their own contexts.

As editor, I share these chapters with some trepidation. Our sample is small and includes only a few voices, experiences, and perspectives. The stories and voices collected here are neither a scientific sample, nor a cross-section that captures the full richness of the diversity of the Episcopal experience. Most (though not all) of the writers are white, middle-class, and from the East

---

2. The EPPN is a part of The Episcopal Church Office of Government Relations located in Washington, DC. The actions, programs, and ministry of the Office of Government Relations are based entirely on policies approved by the Church meeting in General Convention or by the Executive Council. It is a grassroots network of Episcopalians across the country dedicated to carrying out the Baptismal Covenant call to "strive for justice and peace" through the active ministry of public policy advocacy. See http://advocacy.episcopalchurch.org.
3. See http://www2.ed.gov/about/overview/fed/10facts/index.html?exp (accessed November 1, 2016).

Coast. They were invited to contribute their stories to this book because they were connected to the emerging network known as All Our Children.

In these chapters, we hear the voices of preachers, teachers, and ordinary believers who are volunteers, clergy, coalition leaders, and bishops. They are faithfully responding to the guidance of the Holy Spirit as best they understand it, building relationships with their neighbors, listening with open hearts, and seeking to be of service. We hear from founders and leaders of long-term partnerships who have developed thick and transformative ties with their local communities. We hear from volunteers who are just starting out.

These chapters tell the stories of Christians, and their worshipping communities, who practice hospitality, seek to see God's face in people different from themselves, and build the habit of openness among their members. These Christians are living their answers to the question of the church's role in education justice from the particularity of their local context and circumstances. They are "the church" living out its call to be an agent of culture change, helping build just systems of public education. These are ordinary people doing extraordinary things, because they have listened, heard, and responded to the Holy Spirit. They have stepped out to follow Jesus into their neighborhoods. And they have been changed along the way.

Each story is unique, and I hope their particularity opens an invitation for you to seek your own way to connect, respond, and discover how this journey is unfolding in your own life, congregation, and community. I hope they spark many rich conversations and inspire action that in turn elicit more stories that contribute to the church embracing more fully the movement for education equity.

Volunteer-Based Partnerships

Any exploration of volunteer-based partnerships between churches and schools would be incomplete without reflecting on the implications of the dynamics of unequal social power that usually exists between the church and the school in a partnership. The race and power differentials between a congregation—often suburban and white—and a school—often urban and black or Latino—where that congregation is seeking to "make a difference" can be treacherous. To explore them we need more precise language to describe the different ways people offer to help one another.

Emergency help is the right response to natural disasters. *Toxic charity*[4] can maintain the power imbalance and encourage learned helplessness. *Mutuality* is when we get to know one another and take action together out of our shared context. Victims of floods and earthquakes require emergency aid in the form of food, shelter, and medical care. Toxic charity is sometimes motivated by the donor's ego needs, often assumes a deficit model, and usually perpetuates unequal social power, keeping in place the very structures that contributed to the problem. The partnerships between churches and schools that we advocate and celebrate exemplify mutuality.

When volunteers paint school libraries, help teachers and staff with back-to-school nights, or fill backpacks with school supplies, what sort of assistance are they giving? Is it emergency, mutuality, or does it run the risk of being toxic? This is an important question for church volunteers to ask and answer, and it's not always straightforward.

One-time service projects and donation-based relationships can be a point of entry for volunteers, a little like pausing to chat with your neighbor who's out on her front porch. It's a visit with a light touch, which may or may not lead to—or be part of—a deeper relationship. It's a good way to decide if you want to get to know one another better, to build a little trust and familiarity. But for a deeper relationship of mutuality to grow, your neighbor needs to invite you in, and you need to accept. You need to exchange hospitality, which needs to go in both directions.

Serving the children is the purpose, of course, but to make lasting change in community culture, adults surrounding the children need to form bonds of trust and mutuality. One-time service opportunities need to lead to longer-term actions and commitments that are mutually empowering, reciprocal, and transformative for everyone. Connecting volunteers—residents, neighbors, civic leaders, and voters—with the schools thickens community relationships and extends the community's capacity to respond to their local need with locally appropriate response. Sometimes donation-based and direct service opportunities coexist within the context of other longer-term more

---

4. Robert D. Lupton, *Toxic Charity: How Churches and Charities Hurt Those They Help, (And How to Reverse It)* (New York: Harper Collins, 2011). See also *Doing Good . . . Says Who? Stories from Volunteers, Nonprofits, Donors, and Those They Want to Help* by Connie Newton and Fran Early (Minneapolis: Two Harbors Press, 2015).

relationally based partnership work. One way or another a partnership that is growing in mutuality will deepen over time and become more complex, more multilayered. If it does not, that should be a cue for the congregation to check its assumptions about its privilege and learn more about toxic charity.

In addition to the danger of toxic charity, there is another caveat about the role of volunteers we need to navigate. While volunteers can make a difference in a child's life, and a congregation can make a difference in a school, partnerships of volunteers cannot create excellent schools or excellent school systems. The collective volunteer capacity of our country is not sufficient to fill in the gaps in services left by decades of severe budget cuts. Volunteers cannot calm the chaos of a school that has too few experienced teachers and too many needy students. Most volunteers are not trained to heal a traumatized child, and it's hard to hold volunteers accountable, as we must all who work with children. This is important for us to name, because the responsibility for closing the resource allocation gaps sits squarely with the elected and appointed officials of our local and state education agencies. Volunteers learn about these gaps firsthand through their relationships with children, teachers, and staff in the schools. What they learn can change the questions they ask, and it can lead to changes in how they spend their money, and how they vote. Volunteers who allow themselves to be changed can help change the culture by exercising their civic right and responsibility to advocate for solutions within the political process.

While very little research has been done on the measurable benefit of partnerships between churches and public schools, evidence is clear that schools with strong community relationships have better school climates, which correlates with improved student learning. So one argument in favor of church-school partnerships is indirect: because they are good for schools, for families, and communities, they are good for students. Many of these partnerships evolve over time from relatively simple (and sometimes patronizing) one-way relationships of donating goods and services (food, books, help with school events) to the more complex and mutually transformative relationships nurtured by ongoing and longer term commitments (mentoring, multiyear tutoring, spending an hour or two a week in a teacher's classroom for an entire school year). A few partnerships have responded to local circumstances and grown into multilayered, intergenerational, cross-faith coalitions that are bringing new life to their communities.

Why Education Advocacy Is the Church's Mission

While it is beyond the scope of this book to offer a full theology of public education advocacy, the Episcopal Church's foundation in Scripture, tradition, and reason (our "three-legged stool") points to resources the Church can draw on as a starting point for education advocacy, and I want to highlight why this is a theological imperative.

Scripture

Several major scriptural themes are salient for us. Isaiah tells us we will know God's hand is at work when captives are released,[5] which can refer to releasing the constraints of ignorance and bondage. The prophet Jeremiah repeats God's call to seek the welfare of the city in which we dwell,[6] and Micah calls believers to initiate positive action for justice.[7] Paul's vision of the Body of Christ as a physical body, with vulnerable and dishonorable parts that are welcomed and honored, is an image of human community as revolutionary and countercultural in our day of gated communities as it was in first-century Rome. Then as now, the church understands community not as uniformity, but as unity through diversity.[8]

Tradition

Education has been a core value from the earliest days of the Church, because literacy allowed people to study God's word. Christian monastic communities kept learning alive in Europe during the Middle Ages, and during its expansion from the eighteenth through the early twentieth centuries, the Anglican Communion founded schools and universities wherever it became established.

---

5. The spirit of the Lord God is upon me, because the Lord has anointed me; he has sent me to bring good news to the oppressed, to bind up the broken-hearted, to proclaim liberty to the captives, and release for the prisoners (Isa. 61:1).

6. But seek the welfare of the city where I have sent you into exile, and pray to the Lord on its behalf, for in its welfare you will find your welfare (Jer. 29:7).

7. What does the Lord require of you but to do justice, and to love kindness, and to walk humbly with your God? (Mic. 6:8).

8. For just as the body is one and has many members, and all the members of the body, though many, are one body, so it is with Christ. . . . If one member suffers, all suffer together with it; if one member is honored, all rejoice together with it (1 Cor. 12:12, 26).

Reason

The centuries-old Anglican commitment to reason as the third leg of our stool means we value research, history, and facts. It is in this spirit that this book has been assembled for you and the Church. This book is the fruit of research, reflection, and observation, as well as much prayer. We have learned from and with one another, we have benefitted from the work of many—both within the Church and outside it—who have come before us. We have applied our minds as best we can to the challenge we face. We pray the light of knowledge will guide our footsteps and that this book will be a step along the path.

Lallie B. Lloyd
All Saints Day, 2016

CHAPTER ONE

A Social Movement for Education Justice

Lallie B. Lloyd

Low-income children of color are at the epicenter of injustice in our society, and it will take nothing short of a social movement to break this cycle and transform our schools and communities.

> —Mark Warren, "Transforming Public Education: The Need for an Educational Justice Movement"

A National Crisis

After decades of underfunding, high-stakes testing, and increased racial and income segregation, public education in the United States now has two systems of education: one for children of affluence (who are largely white) and one for children of poverty (who are largely black, Latino, or recent immigrants). These two systems are almost completely separate and vastly unequal. The promise of *Brown v. Board of Education* has never been fulfilled, and many agree that this education crisis is the civil rights issue of our time.

Robert Putnam has amply demonstrated that children born into poverty used to be able to benefit from public and community programs that would guide and support them toward long-term well-being. In recent decades so many public and community programs and resources have been dismantled that this is no longer the case, and children born into poverty today face more daunting challenges to their long-term well-being than thirty years ago.[1]

Education is an essential path on the road from poverty to social stability and self-sufficiency, yet access to this path has been systematically blocked for children of poverty—a disproportionate number of whom are children of color—by historical patterns of structural racism, including school and housing segregation, mortgage redlining, voter suppression, hiring bias, and the redirection of public funds for services, programs, and neighborhood investment away from communities and people of color.

The immediate effect of this crisis is young people, too often black males, stunted by their lack of opportunity and alienated from the dominant culture. This is in part because of the dominant culture's passivity in the face of crisis and its failure to take responsibility for its complicity and greed in keeping the public benefit of the nation's wealth disproportionately to themselves. The social fabric of our democracy frays and wears thin as persistent racial and economic inequity causes resentment and often fuels partisan debates as families are harmed across generations by the long-term impact of substandard schooling.

This moral issue, affecting the lives of children, families, communities, and our nation, calls for attention from the church.

While high school graduation rates in the United States are at an all-time high of 82 percent,[2] that statistic masks signs of deep and persistent trouble. For example:

- The racial achievement gap is dramatic. Black fourth graders scored twenty-six points lower on a national reading assessment than their white peers, while Hispanic fourth graders scored twenty-four points lower, a difference equivalent to about two grade levels.[3]
- Graduation rates for students of color are lower than for white students. During the 2013–2014 school year, 87 percent of white students graduated from high school on time, while 76 percent of Hispanic

---

1. Robert D. Putnam, *Our Kids: The American Dream in Crisis* (New York: Simon & Schuster, 2015).
2. See http://nces.ed.gov/programs/coe/indicator_coi.asp (accessed October 6, 2016).
3. A Look at the Education Crisis: Tests, Standards, and the Future of American Education. Center for American Progress, January 2016, 9.

students and 73 percent of black students earned a high school diploma.[4]

- One in eight students is chronically absent.[5] Missing school increases a student's risk of dropping out of high school, and experiencing poor life outcomes (poverty, poor health, and involvement in the criminal justice system).
- Only around 40 percent of high school graduates are prepared for college-level work.[6]
- The correlation between neighborhood income and school quality means schools serving high proportions of children of affluence receive more support, both in funding and in parental and community engagement than those serving high proportions of children in poverty.
- In twenty-three states, high poverty districts spend fewer total dollars per student than low poverty districts, because education funding formulas amplify differences in opportunity instead of ameliorating them.[7]

The root causes of this education crisis are the subject of research and debate among education policy experts. Some experts point to structural and technical problems internal to the education system, such as the length of the school day, high-stakes testing, class size, teacher unions, or the teacher shortage.[8] Arthur Camins describes the position of others who point to social and cultural changes over the last decades:

---

4. Ibid., 9.

5. Defined as missing fifteen or more days of school. See http://www2.ed.gov/datastory /chronicabsenteeism.html (accessed August, 22, 2016)

6. Ulrich Boser, Perpetual Baffour, and Steph Vela, *A Look at the Education Crisis: Tests, Standards, and the Future of American Education* (Washington, DC: Center for American Progress, January 2016), https://cdn.americanprogress.org/wp-content/uploads/2016/01/21075127 /TUDAreport.pdf (accessed October 6, 2016).

7. Center for American Progress, "A Fresh Look at School Funding," https://www .americanprogress.org/issues/education/reports/2015/05/18/113397/a-fresh-look-at-school -funding/ (accessed October 14, 2016).

8. See https://www.washingtonpost.com/news/answer-sheet/wp/2015/08/24/the-real-reasons -behind-the-u-s-teacher-shortage/ (accessed August 22, 2016).

There is no denying that education falls short. However, supporters of equity and democracy need to reframe what ails American education and offer unifying solutions that give people something new to fight for together. . . . The crisis we face in education is not about test scores. Rather, it is that we cannot achieve satisfactory results amidst the far broader crisis of growing inequality, eroding democracy, and escalating divisiveness.[9]

Residential housing patterns are more racially and economically homogenous within themselves and isolated from one another. Affiliative and community-based connections to our neighbors are fractured, and as a nation we have retreated from the consensus that poverty and race should not limit a child's access to quality education.

Education equity, or education justice (the terms are interchangeable), means an education that gives equal opportunity for quality of life to each child. In real life, differences in maternal nutrition, prenatal care, early childhood education, and relative stresses of living in poverty with its correlates of violence, depression, and ill health, mean that children born into poverty often begin life with developmental deficits that require more support—intentional, planned, and publicly funded—than do their more affluent peers. Giving each child an equal opportunity may mean giving different levels of support and services to children in different circumstances. Equality and equity are related, but distinct.

An image may be helpful. Picture three children watching a ball game over a picket fence. In the middle is the older brother, tall and lanky, on his right is the younger sister, and on his left their younger brother. The tall boy in the middle can see over the fence with his feet on the ground. His sister needs a box to see over the fence, and their littlest brother needs two boxes. This is an image of *equity*: they all have what they need to watch the game. *Equality* would mean each child standing on a box of the same size: big brother towers over the fence, sister can barely see, but little brother can't see a thing.[10]

_____

9. See http://www.huffingtonpost.com/arthur-camins/three-strategies-fair-div_b_10361118.html (accessed September 21, 2016).
10. To see the image by Angus Maguire described here, go to http://interactioninstitute.org /illustrating-equality-vs-equity (accessed October 17, 2016).

The education justice we long for is both simple and complex. To paraphrase John Dewey, we want for all children what we want for our own: that they be safe, known, and nurtured; that they be respectful, kind, and know how to share; that they be curious explorers and creative artists; that they learn to think clearly, to interrogate their sources, and plumb the riches of the diverse cultures around them so that the fullness of their own selves might be the gift to the world that God intended.

Parents, teachers, educators, and researchers can describe what this kind of education looks like. Their lists may vary, but here are some things that appear on most of them:

- High quality early childhood education, and universal public pre-K
- Safe, calm, and purposeful school climate
- High and clear academic expectations, accompanied by:
  - High social and academic support
  - Testing that informs classroom instruction
  - The arts and physical education
  - English as a second language instruction
- Social and emotional support:
  - School-based medical and social services
  - Screening, and intervention, and treatment for learning and developmental needs
  - Professional teaching staff
  - Stable, skilled, and supported teaching staff
- Community engagement:
  - Active and broad parent and community engagement in school activities, policy, and leadership
- Meaningful use of out-of-school time:
  - Long-term relationships with caring adults outside the family
  - After-school and summer programs with adult supervision of peer interaction and academic support.

"It's important not to confuse inequity with ineptitude," writes Jack Schneider, summing up the point I'm making here. He says:

The public-education system is undeniably flawed. Yet many of the deepest flaws have been deliberately cultivated. Funding inequity and racial segregation, for instance, aren't byproducts of a system that broke. They are direct consequences of an intentional concentration of privilege. Placing the blame solely on teacher training, or the curriculum, or on the design of the high school—alleging "brokenness"—perpetuates the fiction that all schools can be made great without addressing issues of race, class, and power. This is wishful thinking at its most pernicious.[11]

Thus while structural and technical improvements may help at the margins, if we don't address the cultural challenges—our attitudes, beliefs, and assumptions—the technical changes will be window dressing—as likely to distract us and disguise the real nature of the problem as to reveal it and direct our attention toward solutions.

A Problem of Power

Mark Warren, in his 2014 article "Transforming Public Education: The Need for an Educational Justice Movement,"[12] frames the education crisis as a problem of power. People with social power demand quality schools for their children. They organize around their schools, hold school leaders accountable, and use relational networks to share information about how the system works. People who are marginalized by prejudice based on race, poverty, language, or status often have less social power, limited knowledge, and weaker networks to get their children the schools they need.[13]

> The concept of oppression and terms like *power* are seldom invoked in the mainstream discourse on education reform. Yet, in the end, educational inequality is rooted in and systematically connected to social, economic, and political inequalities in U.S. society. Education reform, then, cannot be considered mainly in technical or organizational terms but rather should be addressed as a profoundly political problem.[14]

---

11. Jack Schneider, "America's Not-So-Broken Education System: Do U.S. Schools Really Need to Be Disrupted?" *The Atlantic,* June 22, 2016, http://www.theatlantic.com/education/archive/2016/06/everything-in-american-education-is-broken/488189/.

12. Mark R. Warren, "Transforming Public Education: The Need for an Educational Justice Movement" *New England Journal of Public Policy* 26, Issue 1, Article 11 (2014), http://scholarworks.umb.edu/nejpp/vol26/iss1/11.

13. Ibid, 7.

14. Ibid.

Warren argues that equity requires transformational change, by which he means changes in the norms, values, and assumptions that undergird the more conscious choices leaders make; in other words, Warren argues for culture change. Changes in policy, practice, or program will bring about only transactional—or more superficial—change, but they cannot change attitudes and beliefs.

Warren defines this social movement for education justice, as a "collective action by oppressed or marginalized people to build power to win changes in government policy and public attitudes that advance the cause of social justice."[15] He and others have documented that such a social movement is already underway in cities as diverse as Oakland, Boston, San Antonio, Chicago, and Denver among many others. Broad-based organizing coalitions that engage parents, youth, teachers, community leaders, and faith-based organizations have been growing for years.[16] All have emerged from their local contexts, and some are affiliated with national networks in the PICO, Gamaliel, and IAF traditions.[17] They are building a movement on the core principles of community organizing: local leadership development, realistic and achievable outcomes, robust coalitions across social barriers, public claims-making based on legal protections, and accountability for officials.

These coalitions are changing the culture within schools and communities. They call for, lead, and support individual and collective acts of cross-boundary speech, assembly, and collaboration, and develop—and then follow—the leadership of parents, teachers, and young people.

---

15. Ibid, 8.
16. See, for example, Mark R. Warren, Karen L. Mapp, and Community Organizing and School Reform Project's *A Match on Dry Grass: Community Organizing as a Catalyst for School Reform* (New York: Oxford University Press, 2011), and Kavitha Mediratta and Seema Shah's *Community Organizing for Stronger Schools: Strategies and Successes* (Cambridge: Harvard University Press, 2009).
17. The Industrial Areas Foundation (IAF), founded in 1940, partners with local religious congregations and civic organizations to build broad-based organizing projects, which create new leadership capacity and citizen-led action (see industrialareasfoundation.org); Gamaliel, founded in 1968, was restructured in 1986 into a leadership institute that trains community leaders to build and maintain powerful organizations in low-income communities (see gamaliel.org); the PICO National Network (formerly the Pacific Institute for Community Organizations) was founded in 1972. In the PICO model, congregations serve as the institutional base for community organizations (see piconetwork.org).

Community-based leadership development, parental engagement, youth and teacher activism, and local accountability are among the practices effecting the requisite culture change that can bring about the "high-quality humane schools" Warren reminds us we all want for all our children.

Warren names three ways social movements change arrangements of unequal power: they demand recognition, use their collective voice, and stimulate broad participation. These movements can change attitudes and reframe the public conversation; they challenge the negative stereotypes faced by children of color in school, on the streets, and in the media.[18] Today the church is joining its neighbors in demanding recognition, asserting a collective voice, and participating broadly in many places, including volunteer-based partnerships.

Today's Social Movements

Social movements transform the people who join and build them, bridging the silos of race and class around shared vision and purpose. Today's social movement for education justice provides churches a "way in" to engage effectively and confidently with local schools. While the church has something to contribute to this movement, it also has much to gain. This is good news for churches and other communities of faith that feel called to work for education justice, because this movement is grounded in the crucial democratic principles of inclusion, local leadership, transparency, and full participation.

Relationships nurtured through collective action toward shared purpose, based on research, and developing local democratic participation are crucial to reweave the fabric of our democracy. Community organizing coalitions build relationships with local leaders and other advocates that multiply one congregation's impact, and organizations like the Education Law Center,[19] the Education Trust,[20] and the Annie E. Casey Foundation[21] generate high quality data that congregations could not acquire on their own.[22]

---

18. Warren (on page 8) gives credit to Jeannie Oakes and John Rogers from *Learning Power: Organizing for Education and Justice* (New York: Teachers College Press, 2005).

19. See www.edlawcenter.org.

20. See www.edtrust.org.

21. See www.aecf.org.

22. The Episcopal Church's Office of Research and Statistics also compiles demographic, income, and employment information on the communities around every congregation. See www.episcopalchurch.org/page/research-and-statistics.

Church-school partnerships benefit from research into educational history, policy and best practice, as well as social systems thinking, which can equip them to "get up on the balcony" from where we can see how the interwoven connections of race, poverty, and policy contribute to our education crisis. Learning how to connect the dots between federal housing mortgage insurance, redlining, "ghettos," black urban poverty and white affluent suburbs, and "good" and "bad" schools changes our understanding of these complex issues. It invites us to ask and explore different questions and challenges us to acknowledge any unearned benefit we may have received and to seek to ameliorate the harm done on our behalf.

Social movements are strengthened when those of us who have benefitted from historical patterns of injustice commit to becoming effective allies, build relationships, and contribute time and energy to make the necessary changes in policies and practices. Beneficiaries of unearned privilege due to race and class must make both individual and corporate acts of repentance and take responsibility for the harm done by historic patterns of racism and greed. Not in order to control the movement, but to learn from it, be changed by it and strengthen it. The church is called to join this social movement for education justice to heal our own divisions and because Christians believe broken relationships can be healed through repentance and just action. We have words to speak and actions to take that can help.

The words the church speaks matter: the stories we tell, the hope we proclaim, the promises we repeat. These words open hearts, sometimes bringing hope and refreshment, and sometimes convicting a conscience.

The world sorely needs to hear the messages our liturgical practices and rituals proclaim in action and symbol. We set a public table and proclaim that God invites all to approach; we light a candle in the darkness and proclaim that life has overcome death; we wash one another's feet as a reminder that we are called to servant ministry. We leave the table nourished and equipped to bear God's gifts of healing and reconciliation, which were not given to the church for the church's own sake. They were and are given—moment by moment—to the church for the sake of the whole world.

Our acts of holding, speaking, and acting can be transformative acts that change culture; they are not merely technical or structural fixes. They are social acts, requiring and nurturing connection with others, and the transformation is mutual. It goes in both directions. We do not serve another at the sacred meal without opening to the possibility of transformation. We do not mentor a child without being changed. Our practice and our words change lives, and those lives change the people around them.

Culture Change

If the root causes of the current education crisis are the subject of research and debate among education policy experts, what the Church can and is doing about it is the subject of this book.

Church leaders are calling attention to the moral crisis of the education opportunity gap and the school-to-prison pipeline, to their root causes in implicit race bias, and the impact of historical patterns of structural racism, and the overall recognition that concerns of people of color in general—and black people in particular—do not get the attention they deserve.

What does the Church bring to the table of public education advocacy?

Alexia Salvatierra and others claim that we as church have a unique voice, perspective, and role to play in our local justice movements and that if we do not participate, our gifts may not be available to our friends and allies who need them.[23] For example, she points out that Christians are drawn forward by hope.[24] We believe God is not finished yet. Scripture teaches us that creation is not finished, that Jesus had many more things to teach us than he had time for, and that the story ends in the beautiful City of God, where there will be no more tears.

As Christians, we are motivated to make change not only because we reject the bad things we see around us. In our lived experience—in our hearts and lives—we know resurrection. Alexia reminds us we are drawn forward toward the fulfilled promise of new life, of being reborn, of forgiveness and reconciliation.[25] We believe justice is part of God's dream, so our confidence goes beyond wishful thinking or naiveté, but rests on the eternal nature of the Creator, robust and solid.

---

23. Alexia Salvatierra and Peter Heltzel, *Faith-Rooted Organizing: Mobilizing the Church in Service to the World* (Downers Grove, IL: InterVarsity Press, 2014). 105.

24. Ibid., 84.

25. Ibid., 34–38.

When we join the movement for education justice, we bring with us this precious commodity of hope, a gift to share with our neighbors and allies.[26] Participating in this urgent and challenging work draws on the fullness of our moral resources, collective resiliency, and hope.

We are called to be a keeper of the memory (our history, narrative, and stories of how we came to be here, and a community of the Dream of God. Seeking that all creation will live together in peace and harmony draws us forward from our present incompleteness. As church, we hold an attractive hope for the future. Being repulsed by realities of the present moment or arguing about what's bad and who is at fault is not the mission to which God calls us. We know that emerging reality needs to be cocreated with neighbors—and we know we don't own this vision, it's God's, and God wants all the nations—all the people—participating in it. So at our best the church enters conversations and takes action for quality public education in an open-hearted, socially inviting, hospitable, curious stance toward our neighbors. Who else is here, with whom we can partner, to work for quality education in our community?

It is this trifold potential to connect broad-based community activism and engagement (the hands and feet of local service and action) with the fluency of research, systems thinking, and policy frames (the head of historical patterns), and with the power and energy of personal connections (the heart of relationships) that gives unique power to faith communities in advocating for education justice. Cultural change happens when large segments of the country reframe the nature of a problem and reveal the values and beliefs that invisibly undergird the choices and decisions that are visible. Cultural change addresses the invisible mindsets, mental models, and unconscious narratives that perpetuate the visible programs, policies, and practices.

Cultural change is, therefore, the business of religion: making the Dream of God a reality.

---

26. One example of a Christian bringing hope in the face of challenge is Sara Jane Walker's story of community-based relational justice work in her article, "Walking the Children to School: A Neighborhood Story" *Journal of Missional Practice* (Spring 2016): http://journalof missionalpractice.com/walking-the-children (accessed October 14, 2016).

CHAPTER TWO

Why We're Here

Diana Carson

If we are to love our neighbors, before doing anything else we must see our neighbors.

—Frederick Buechner, *Whistling in the Dark*

W hy don't we go around the table and each say our name and why we're here, OK?"

Adina Schecter looks around the table at us, smiling. It's our first official team check-in with Adina S., literacy coach at the McCormack Middle School, something to help us library volunteers get to know each other even better. We've already been working together for a couple of months.

OK, I think, why am I here? I look at my fellow volunteers. We've all said yes to the library project here. Can I actually share my answer aloud with the group? I am here because I think this could be the chance I have been praying for.

My journey to the McCormack Middle School in the Boston neighborhood of Dorchester started over a networking coffee with Louise Packard, executive director of the Trinity Boston Foundation. After thirteen years in the leafy suburbs raising our two children, I was more than ready to work outside the home again. Louise is a friend who knows a lot of people in the nonprofit sector in Boston. We first met when I was working for Trinity Church Boston on their website redesign back in 2001, and we had recently reconnected in a neighborhood Bible study group. At Starbucks she listened to my story, my desire to contribute to the wider world through mission-driven work. She gave me a few names. Then she mentioned a possible library project at the McCormack. "Why don't you go down there and check things out?" she suggested.

I wasn't sure about working in a middle school in Dorchester—it seemed too far away geographically, and far from what I was familiar with. I had taught middle schoolers, but most of that work had been in private schools, to kids of my own demographic: white and privileged. The students at the McCormack Middle School were among those of the highest need in the city, mostly of color, and a significant number were homeless. In my twenty-five years of living in greater Boston I had spent very little time in Dorchester. My considerable volunteer hours as a stay-at-home parent were spent almost exclusively within my own suburban community—in church and in my kids' schools.

The professional experience and skills that fellow parents brought to our local PTA were impressive. And this was "normal" in the 'burbs: moms with MBAs running school auctions to raise tens of thousands of dollars for new computers and smart boards; architect dads designing playgrounds; engineers organizing robotics clubs and teaching kids after school; science fairs, debate clubs, school newspapers.

They also had great school libraries, staffed by large teams of parent volunteers and managed by professional librarians—all for kids who didn't always need to use a library, because their parents ordered the books they wanted on Amazon Prime.

"Social capital" is the term I had heard Marshall Ganz of the Harvard Kennedy School use to describe these kinds of resources available within a community. People—parents, grandparents, and friends—are able and willing to share their time, talent, networks, and in many instances, their money to optimize their kids' education.

I knew from working briefly on a writing project for Citizen Schools[27] that parent involvement of this kind was a hallmark of affluent suburban

---

27. Citizen Schools partners with public middle schools in low-income communities to provide an expanded learning day. See http://www.citizenschools.org.

schools, a luxury many took for granted. And that "parent involvement" in a school that served a poor, inner-city population didn't apply in the same way. When parents are working two and three jobs, have limited English proficiency, and are raising kids without a financial safety net, just getting kids to school regularly is a major feat. Forget a PTA.

And even with funding like we have here in Massachusetts (number one in the country in terms of overall quality of our public schools), most schools are not equipped to address student needs that stem from the core issue—poverty. "Food insecurity" outside of the school day, the need for clothing, for healthcare, trauma and the need for safety from violence, and the need for extra help with foundational skills like reading and with homework after school are all outcomes of living in poverty.

You almost can't pick up the *Boston Globe* these days without seeing another article about educational inequity. As it turns out, Boston is ground zero for income disparity: number one in the country. The numbers of very poor people are growing, and the very rich are growing in numbers as well. And the rich and poor are increasingly separated from each other in daily life.

Poor students (mostly African American and Hispanic) are heavily concentrated in the same areas of the city, just the way that affluent students (mostly white) are clustered in certain towns outside the city. And in what seem like two separate, closed systems, all the disadvantages of being poor, and all the advantages of being affluent, multiply and intensify.

I knew all of this before I ever visited the McCormack. I knew about it, and I felt bad about the state of things for the kids in the "wrong" zip codes. The deck was stacked against them. But knowing something intellectually and seeing it up close, personally, are two very different things. Despite my family's modest but meaningful philanthropic contributions to organizations serving the poor in Boston, despite tithing at church and being politically active, I still felt guilty and helpless.

It's a big problem. One writer recently called educational inequity *the* civil rights issue of our time.[28]

---

28. Esther L. Bush. February 27, 2013. See www.whitehouse.gov/blog/2013/02/27/education -civil-rights-issue-our-time.

But what are we to do? It feels overwhelming. The controversy over charter schools versus public schools makes it seem complicated too. The solutions aren't clear-cut. Or are they?

Recently in our Bible study group we had discussed the story of Jesus and the loaves and fishes. I had always read this story to be primarily about the miraculous abundance of the Kingdom of God. Jesus makes plenty of food appear out of nowhere for thousands of hungry people. Awesome—literally! I thought I understood this story; I had it all down. But our group discussion went in a different direction from what I had expected. Could it be, one friend suggested, that the miracle was the spirit of generosity among the people present that day? That instead of Jesus distributing the food to the masses, the people themselves reached into their own pockets and shared everything they had with their neighbors? Kind of like that folktale "Stone Soup."[29] Sharing what you have. Maybe that's the miracle. The Holy Spirit inspiring people to work the miracle. It was so simple, but I grasped the story in a new way. And something shifted in the way I saw my possible role in the world. Who knows, I thought, maybe they could use me at the McCormack.

I decided to make a visit and followed through with Rainey Dankel, associate rector of social justice at Trinity—in the spirit of "just showing up" for stuff in life (Woody Allen). Soon Rainey and I were zipping down I-93, chatting about how bad Boston drivers are. And she filled me in on Trinity Boston Foundation's presence at the McCormack, in the form of embedded counselors on-site. Many of the students have experienced trauma in their daily lives outside of school, and this trauma leads to behavioral issues at school. The key to interrupting the on-ramp to prison, she explained, was the restorative justice model in which students who disrupt classes and act out aren't suspended or expelled. They are brought together with those whom they have offended, and everyone is helped to listen and talk it over. The offending students get individual counseling. There is communication, understanding, and redemption. There are second chances. There are many chances.

A light rain drizzled from a gray sky that day as we pulled up to the building. As many public schools do, the exterior of the building looked grim and uninviting. Across the street stood the housing development (a "project") where the first McCormack students lived.

---

29. Marcia Brown, *Stone Soup* (New York: Simon & Schuster, 1947).

Adina Davidson, clinical manager for school culture, met us at the door with a big smile and a warm handshake. She took us around the school, introducing us to friendly teachers and filling us in: the highest incidence of homelessness of any school in Boston, over 75 percent of students under the poverty line, many in foster care, more than half English language learners (ELL) and recent immigrants, no librarian ever, and no library since 2010. (I have since learned that over half of Boston public schools have no professional librarians.) Many of the students were there because they had been kicked out of other schools for bad behavior. The others were there because their parents did not have the resources to negotiate the city's lottery process. "This is a sad place. Nobody wants their kid to end up here," she said plainly. Her honesty was disarming. The school building was dark and dreary, with no center to its structure, no heart. Voices echoed loudly off tile walls in between classes, and every hallway looked the same.

A stop into the Trinity Boston Foundation counselors' office brought the chance to meet a few students and see the staff in action. I learned that this office was the only trauma-sensitive space available to students in the school. There were soft chairs, some rugs, and a few colorful posters on the walls.

Two girls looked like they were sleeping in the corner on beanbag chairs. "They don't sleep at night," Adina whispered. The "life coach" on staff was talking on the phone about housing options for a student. A counselor was giving a girl with short hair in a flannel shirt what sounded like a pep talk and encouraging her to watch Rachel Maddow on TV, because she was powerful and confident, with great style. "You will love her jackets!" she said. Rainey and I chimed in about how we liked to watch Rachel Maddow on TV too, and the student smiled and gave us high-fives as we left. We were in her safe space, and I guess we were OK by association with the counselors. It was an unexpected moment of connection.

We moved on to a meeting with the two teachers: Adina Schecter, literacy coach, and Neema, social studies teacher. They were the ones with a plan to create a new library in the school. The goal, they explained, was to create a culture of reading at the McCormack. Many McCormack students don't have access to books in their homes, and it was unlikely they used their local public library. But reading for pleasure has been linked to better educational outcomes for students. Adina mentioned a British study that found that the amount of reading for pleasure a student does between the ages of ten and sixteen is a bigger factor in her educational success than her parents' academic achievement. An accessible library could make a big difference.

Adina and Neema needed arms and legs to make their vision a reality— the library project was something they had pursued on the side. They explained what it would take and showed us the space: a large room with boxes of books strewn about. Someone would need to sort, tag, and catalog all the books. There would be new books delivered soon—they had written a grant proposal and received funds from the Laura Bush Foundation. Eventually they would need people to staff the library and possibly tutor students.

Adina talked about how libraries differ from classrooms: they give students a place for independent inquiry, to explore their own curiosities and interests. She referred to Ta-Nehisi Coates's formative experience of unlimited access to books, choosing his own reading, and reading for pleasure as recounted in *Between the World and Me*.[30] Yes, of course, I realized, all students deserved the opportunity to read for pleasure.

"Think about how you might like to be involved," she said with a warm smile, as she escorted us to the door.

At that point I had heard the facts, I had seen the building, I had even met some kids and staff: the friendly, welcoming teachers in the hallways, City Year[31] staff, Citizen Schools.[32] And the messy room with all the books that could have been on a reality TV show about hoarding. At this point, I could have very appropriately thanked Adina Davidson for her time, praised everyone's efforts, and driven away without making any commitments, still wondering what this all really had to do with me. Too much to take on right now. Not really my thing. Too long a commute.

But Adina Davidson turned to me and asked, "So, what are you thinking? How does this all feel to you, seeing the school?" And she waited for me to answer.

And I did: "This is so different from what my own kids have in their schools. And it's not right."

---

30. Ta-Nehisi Coates, *Between the World and Me* (New York: Random House, 2015).
31. See https://cityyear.org.
32. See http://www.citizenschools.org.

And that was it: my moment of conversion. I went from spectator to participant in two sentences. And if she had never asked me for a reaction, I don't know how it all might have gone differently. I might have been able to get back into the car and drive home, to a world away from this neighborhood, and not get involved. But as soon as I was asked to react to what I was seeing in front of me, the students who were in some almost forgotten place where the rest of the world had given up on them, the students with big problems, on the on-ramp to prison, born in the "wrong" zip code, where, as James Baldwin says, "You were not expected to aspire to excellence: you were expected to make peace with mediocrity."[33]

I realized I couldn't be OK with it all. I was angry. I had to do something. And now I was part of the library project.

Compassion is the sometimes fatal capacity for feeling what it's like to live in someone else's skin. It's the knowledge that there can never really be any peace and joy for me until there is peace and joy finally for you too.[34]

I started to reach out to friends and invited them down to work on the library. We would be digging into the unsorted books—hundreds of them—to create some order. I framed it in an e-mail as an opportunity to give back. Several friends from my town and my kids' school were very interested and thanked me for reaching out. And there were some Trinity folks who came that first day and all the workdays to follow. The people who responded to the call for volunteers at the McCormack were not working full-time during the day and so had the luxury of time, among other forms of privilege. But they were craving meaningful work. One friend said she had been looking for a chance to see an inner-city school library, and wanted to donate money before the end of the calendar year. It was December eighth. The timing made the hair on the back of my neck stand on end.

We were of different ages and backgrounds, but all of us had the ability to commit to some weekday hours at this school. We shared snacks and helped each other figure stuff out. Teachers at the school visited us and expressed their gratitude, as did a few students.

33. James Baldwin, *The Fire Next Time* (New York: Random House, 1993), 7.
34. Frederick Buechner, *Wishful Thinking* (New York: Harper & Row, 1973), 18.

Over the course of four weeks in December, we brought order to the room and got a start on entering the books into a catalog system.

In January we were in a holding pattern while the staff decided how they wanted to proceed. There was still administrative work to do. There was talk of tutoring students, book groups. Then in February, we were invited back to continue the administrative work and start working with groups of students on Tuesday and Thursday afternoons. The library shelves had been assembled by teachers and staff, there was carpeting and some beautiful large armchairs. We were told that the students at the school loved the space. A small group of students had visited recently and were so surprised and happy to see their new library. One of the girls had said incredulously, "Why do we have this? What did we do to deserve this?"

We are doing more than creating a space for students to check out books and helping them read more. That is all good and very important, for sure. But we are also helping to send a message to the students that they are important, they matter, and their learning is important.

I will never forget an encounter one day with an eighth-grade boy who had recently visited the library and found a book that spoke to him. In fact, he was carrying it around everywhere he went. It was a book of poetry by Tupac Shakur. Adina introduced the student to me and other library volunteers in the hallway between classes, and he quickly pulled out the book and showed us his favorite poem. That moment inspires me to keep up my work as a volunteer in the library.

The irony seems to be that even though working at the McCormack means that I see and hear things that make me sad and remind me of the brokenness and injustice of the world, being there also gives me hope. I guess this is the joy to be found in vocation that Parker Palmer[35] wrote about. I am hopeful that the boys and girls at the school will get a fair shot at happiness and success: that they will love reading and books; that the library will be a source of comfort to them. And who knows what more?

Now, sitting around the table with the other library volunteers, I quickly try to compose an answer to "Why are you here?"

---

35. Parker Palmer, *Let Your Life Speak: Listening for the Voice of Vocation* (San Francisco: John Wiley & Sons, 2000), 16.

"I am here because Louise asked me to check it out," I say lightly, and others smile and nod. I have chickened out, trying to not be too intense. But there are others at the table who are bold in their comments.

"I feel like I am finally really living out my faith in this work," a man says enthusiastically.

I hear a friend talking about how much this volunteer job means to her. She says shyly, "I've always wanted to teach and work with kids after earning my MEd, but after having three kids, I didn't have time for a job. But now, I don't know, maybe this is a calling for me, or something."

A retired librarian explains that she loved her work but that it was so long ago. She smiles and shrugs, looking down at her hands on the table. "But maybe I can still do something good here."

I am inspired and admire my friends, new and old. Their words strike a chord in me. The humble yearning, the cautious hope. "Do I belong here? Can I do something good here?"

I have the sense that we share a yearning to answer a call. To help bridge a gap. Finding this work, responding to this need, is for me an experience of being found, in a profound sense—found and claimed by God. It's no mistake that I am here. And as the number of us on the McCormack library team grows, we all are part of something good that feels bigger than any one of us.

A miracle is when the whole is greater than the sum of its parts. A miracle is when one plus one equals a thousand.[36]

September 13, 2016, Postlude:

We finished the 2015–2016 school year with a total of fifteen volunteers. There were 147 students who had checked out books by the end of the school year and the library had over six thousand books. Over the summer, volunteers worked over one hundred hours in sometimes sweltering heat to learn a new catalog system and input all the books again. This year our team has twenty volunteers, and we will staff the library Monday through Thursday. Future plans include a student book review program and an after-school tutoring program. Our goal for the year is to increase student utilization of the library by 30 percent.

---

36. Frederick Buechner. *The Alphabet of Grace* (New York: HarperCollins, 1989), 60.

CHAPTER THREE

Finding Jesus in Unexpected Places

Jackie Whitfield

There is no simple or immediate way to discern the right response without a relationship.

—Robert D. Lupton, *Toxic Charity*

Finding Jesus in unexpected places, taking God's hand to walk in faith along uncharted paths, and taking God's Church into the world had always been part of the DNA of All Saints' Episcopal Church, in Concord, North Carolina. Many thriving ministries in our community had been started on our campus with the leadership and vision of our former leaders. We had seen needs and responded with the founding of the night shelter, battered women's home, the community free clinic, and the food pantry. But as time passed, the memories of standing on the shoulders of giants had faded, and slowly our parish turned more inward, not as active in our community or our diocese. In July 2013, with great sadness, the forty-year-old preschool on our campus closed, because it was no longer financially sound, and its model no longer served the young families in our community.

The silent halls of All Saints' education wing cried out to be filled with children. As our church became more still, an All Saints' Task Force was

created. It was charged with the task of exploring "needs for preschool chil-
dren in our community and mak[ing] a recommendation to the vestry."
At the same time our priest, the Reverend Nancy L. J. Cox, attended com-
munity meetings where questions were posed to all community nonprofits:
"What do you have to offer and what do you need?" Meanwhile, the Most
Reverend Michael B. Curry, at that time our diocesan bishop, continually
preached on going to Galilee as he traveled the diocese. Ironically, All Saints'
Episcopal Church was situated at the crossroads of our community, a modern
Galilee. The Holy Spirit was putting things into motion. The congregation
just needed to listen.

At the nonprofits meeting, the Cabarrus County Schools representative
wrote: "We have preschool children and no room." All Saints' wrote: "We
have preschool space and no children." Ann Benfield, the director of the
Cabarrus Partnership for Children, saw those two notes and moved forward
with scheduling a meeting for these three groups.

In the meantime, the All Saints' Task Force learned that the county had
an annual waiting list of three to four hundred children living in economically challenged homes. These children qualified for preschool subsidies, but
there was no place for them to attend preschool. Without preschool, the children from these homes were entering kindergarten unprepared to learn. Our
congregation listened to this presentation, and then watched a film, *The First
Two Thousand Days of a Child's Life*.[37] The film focused on the importance of
preschool for children born into poverty. Education gave children and their
families hope. It was hard for our parish family to realize that children who
entered school unprepared were most likely to drop out of school, end up
in prison, become teen parents, or drug addicts. How could these sweet and
precious children be so doomed? Doomed at the age of three or four or five.
How horrible. What could All Saints' do to be part of the solution and ensure
equity in education for the quiet and vulnerable children?

All Saints' surrounded these unknown children and families in prayer.
We prayed for divine guidance for our church family. We prayed without
ceasing. Our hearts were softened to meet the need of these silent children in
our community. All Saints' wanted to be part of the solution.

---

37. See www.first2000days.org and http://buildthefoundation.org.

The meetings began with representatives and leaders from Cabarrus County Schools, All Saints', and Cabarrus Partnership for Children. Certainly this was an unlikely partnership; many thought it impossible. Questions arose about finances and the separation of church and state. Building inspections began; we needed to bring our 1980s era education wing up to state building codes and public school standards if we were to house a public preschool. Calls to the Department of Public Instruction asking about public preschool guidelines led to comments of: "This will never work." and "I've never heard of such a thing—a church and public school working together."

Estimates for building updates astounded everyone. It was estimated to cost $500,000 to open a state-certified preschool. To say this seemed impossible to All Saints' and its vestry was an understatement. However, our faithful God was in our midst, the roadblocks began to disappear, and the right people with the right talents showed up in the right places at the right times. The Holy Spirit filled this place and God's people.

By January 2014, our congregation was hearing God's call to cast our nets wide and deep in order to serve God's most fragile children in our county. God's plan was yet to be revealed. Our church family was unaware, but we were about to step out of the boat in faith.

The church needed a contact person: a retired educator, teacher, principal, and lifelong Episcopalian volunteer to be the liaison for this project. Then a young man who had grown up in the church was asked to be the senior warden. Quiet and faithful in demeanor, he hesitatingly accepted the call. In serving in this capacity, his faith deepened, and he was often awestruck at how the Holy Spirit worked through and in him. God changed his life. God changed the life of our congregation.

In March, the chair of the task force made a presentation to All Saints' vestry with the staggering cost of bringing our building up to code. Serving on the vestry, I found this to be a powerful experience of listening, silence, prayer, and then conversation. Those of us on the vestry unanimously agreed that we were responsible for being good stewards of our church resources, and making timely payments on a tremendous building debt. Our reserves were sacred and untouchable. Out of the silence in the room a bold motion was made by one of the most fiscally conservative members of the vestry: "Move all reserves into a building fund line item so the renovations can begin, and we will partner with the Cabarrus County Schools and the Cabarrus

Partnership for Children to open a public preschool for children on our campus." There was silence, then prayer, then a second to the motion, and a call to vote.

The twelve people around the table voted unanimously to move forward. The Holy Spirit moved among us in a powerful way, a way that only the heart can explain. What we lacked in resources, we made up for in our love for our God and God's people. With tears in our eyes, the vestry moved forward, not with a typical "business plan," but with a "faith plan." This was the work of our Triune God: God was with us, God would guide us, God would provide. Our faith would lead us into a world bigger than ourselves. We were called to serve the least among us. Our lives would change forever. Soon the life of our church family would also change.

Communication and transparency were imperative. The *First 2000 Days* film was shown to the congregation. Individuals did research about the demographics of our neighborhoods and discovered there were four hundred children who qualified for subsidized early childhood education in our midst. Parish meetings were held and we made sure we were transparent about costs, who would do the work, and what actually needed to be done. We held monthly, and sometimes weekly, parish meetings. Open conversations were held for people to come, listen, and hear. We reached out to people who were having difficulty with the idea. We addressed tension directly, making a space for it to allow the Holy Spirit to enter. We sought to build capacity and momentum so that everyone could embrace our vision. Prayers encircled the project, the yet-to-be-known children and families we would serve, the inspectors, the construction workers, and our parish family.

During the height of the renovations and negotiations with the school system, the project was led by the wardens, vestry, and a group of dedicated, prayerful, and talented laypeople: architects, construction engineers, retired educators, and volunteers from everywhere. Among the hundreds of volunteers who participated in this project were those who sat in the pews every Sunday, those who were rarely in the pews, those who had walked away from the church, people outside our parish, the young, the old, and sometimes those who were sick. The energy, dedication, and fellowship were electric.

What was happening was bigger than any of us. The church was filled with hope and light. The doors had been flung open, light was pouring in, and our little parish would never be the same.

No work is without the tug and pull of tensions. Fear over finances reared its head on multiple occasions, as did the challenge of sharing space between the soon-to-be preschool and All Saints' Sunday school. And we heard comments such as, "What do you mean we can't teach about Jesus in this school?" Construction deadlines were delayed. Fear would creep in among the faithful.

The tougher the situation, the more we prayed. The prayer warriors, including the Mary Martha Chapter of the Daughters of the King, prayed. The vestry prayed. Everyone prayed.

We applied for a grant in April from the Cannon Foundation. We were told that they "usually didn't give grants of this size to partners at the beginning" of a project. It was going to cost $200,000 to $250,000; the grant would replenish our reserves. In June, after we had committed our reserves to the project, our church was awarded the grant to reimburse our coffers. The money for the education wing updates had been provided to within about $40,000. Another grant and gifts from private donors covered the balance we needed.

In July representatives from All Saints', the Partnership for Children, and the county school district made a presentation to the Cabarrus County School Board, which unanimously accepted the contracts and partnership. They also voted to name the new school after Dr. David A. Lockhart, a former All Saints' parishioner, school board member during the days of school integration in our community, and a beloved pediatrician. Dr. Lockhart had been a man of small stature who was kind, gentle, and peaceful. When he arrived in Concord as a young pediatrician, he saw need in the African American community and opened an office in the Logan Community, which was segregated at the time. He worked for peace and against violence. He started a clinic at a local hospital for children who had been abused sexually, mentally, or physically. As a pediatrician, Dr. Lockhart took care of the whole family and he knew the children in the whole community. It was fitting that The Lockhart Early Learning Center on the All Saints' campus had become the newest school within the Cabarrus County School system. All Saints' resolved to walk the gospel instead of preaching it.

Lawyers walked the halls prior to the opening to make sure there were no visible symbols of Christianity.

God was removing the roadblocks and building bridges.

By late August the project was building to a crescendo. The All Saints' volunteers were physically exhausted. Unexpected tensions arose. Two weeks before school was to begin, some school personnel suddenly learned they had this new school added to their responsibilities. There was tension due to a communication glitch within the school system. (The liaison to the school district didn't tell the support systems—technology, maintenance, and nutrition—back in April when they should have, but waited until the last minute.) It was not always pleasant. Due to deep personal roots within the community, everything that needed to be done got done. All parties resolved to make the partnership work. We persevered and prayed for understanding, peace, courage, and collaboration. Work together we did. After the school opening, we were able to break bread, laugh, and tell stories. We celebrated children and the school.

In September 2014, a year after the closing of our former preschool, the lease and memorandum of understanding between All Saints' and the county school system was signed. The Lockhart Early Learning Center was a reality. Bishop Anne Hodges-Copple blessed the renovated preschool space, and we prayed for the still-unknown children and families who would be the first to enter the school.

That month many happy parents received the phone calls telling them there was a place for their child. Teachers were hired, and an opening date was planned for October. A ribbon-cutting ceremony and dedication was scheduled in November 2014.

Many groups attended the ribbon-cutting: school board members, our local US Congressman Richard Hudson and his staff, the wife and adult children of the late Dr. David A. Lockhart, the Board of the Cannon Foundation, the Board of Cabarrus Partnership for Children, the All Saints' vestry, church members, and many community leaders and volunteers. This was a momentous celebration in our community, as well as a witness to the generosity of our God to faithful people. As one member said, "God used us to accomplish the Spirit's plan. God placed everyone where they were needed. This was way bigger than us! What seemed impossible was made possible."

In the fall of 2016 we entered into our third year of this partnership. Our church has changed. The original twelve vestry members who made the bold decision to hear God's call and move into a "faith model" not a "business model" have seen our lives changed forever. Like Jesus's disciples, we were fearful at times, we heard the nasty remarks, and sometimes we began to sink when we tried to walk on the water.

However, we always believed God would provide and was in our midst. Often we talk with tears in our eyes about how God changed us forever in this experience. We are hungry to share our faith stories, often a little too timid in the sharing. Our sweet Lord has softened our hearts. We are more aware of those who are in need. We are the hands, feet, and heart of Jesus in our community. Most importantly, the families in the Lockhart Center mirror Jesus's love to us. What joy it is to walk beside someone in the journey called life. Our hearts are overflowing with love, compassion, hope, and light.

When we look at the All Saints' congregation today, we see a parish family that is empowered and full of the Holy Spirit. Our congregation is open, welcoming, and becoming more diverse.

One parish member said, "When I look at those filling our pews on Sunday, it is like a glimpse of heaven: where color of skin, place of birth, or sexual orientation no longer divide us. We are all God's people and beloved by God." It has been a wonderful metamorphosis of our church family over the last four years.

Another member said, "During my lunch break, I often park in the church parking lot, roll down my windows, and listen to voices of the children drifting through the air. I give thanks to God for opening our hearts to do this work: a public preschool for children on our church campus, a place for four-year-olds who otherwise would not be in school. I pray for a way for other churches to be called to do this work. I pray to add a building to our campus so more children can attend school." Please God, continue to answer the prayers of your people.

One of our volunteers who assists in maintaining the "Gardens of All Saints'" on our campus comes early in the morning to work and pray. She said that during these quiet times, she often has tender conversations with families, especially young mothers bringing children to school. Some parents have offered to help in the gardens. Other times, she is washed in the Holy Spirit and filled with hope as she hears the children's happy voices.

All Saints' recently realized that 40 percent of the children attending the Lockhart Center are of Latino or Hispanic origin. A parishioner paid to place a statue of Our Lady of Guadalupe in a garden near the sidewalk to the school. Within four days, the statue of Our Lady was decorated with flowers, a beautiful blessing from the F3 (Faith, Fitness, and Fellowship) men who discovered this early one morning while exercising. The men were overcome with the joy of the quiet ministry of being Jesus to the stranger.

The Holy Spirit has moved All Saints': we are a more active, inclusive community of faith. New members have spoken of the energy they feel in our parish. They may not have been part of the actual opening of the school, but they feel bathed in love and hope as a result of this ongoing ministry. They are touched by the stories of the Spirit moving through our congregation to create and support the preschool's opening. One member stated, "I came to church new to the community: a stranger with no friends, feeling alone, and downtrodden. I have no education background, but I am a volunteer at the preschool. I read to the children. At first, I was unaware that some children were not read to at home, so I had to build trust and expectations with them. Now, they are so excited to see me, and they hug me when I leave. We are both filled with hope and happiness. I am so impressed with the teachers, what the children are learning, and how they grow throughout the year. I come to church to be refueled, and during the week, I go into Lockhart so I can love God's children, and they love me. I am overflowing with joy!"

Another new member volunteered to be a literacy tutor for parents. She too was new to our church and was attracted by the congregation's open and loving spirit. She has now been tutoring for six months and has built a loving and trusting partnership with the parents.

"I am so blessed by the ladies who are learning English and to read and write," she said. "They are so thankful to me, and I have become so blessed by them. We are reflecting Jesus's love to each other. I feel we are building a bridge of gratitude, walking beside each other with acceptance. My empty heart is full of *hope* and *love*!"

Our music director/organist was not trained in music education, so when he was asked to teach music to four-year-olds, he became a bit overwhelmed and anxious. He has now completed three summer sessions in the Orff Method of music awareness with children, which he sees as a joyful extension of his music ministry. "I am more open to the love of the Holy Spirit," he says. "And at times I am overwhelmed by the blessings! Children who experience music are more self-confident and respond to directions better. Their creativity and expressions are beautiful. I can't wait to start another year. I have grown as a Christian through this experience."

Our outreach to the school has changed over the years; we are no longer the dispenser of goods, but rather guides and partners supporting people in their walks of life. We walk holding sacred space for the families, sharing love and hope. We are creating a loving and trusting sanctuary.

All Saints' now partners with the Cabarrus Literacy Council to train adult literacy coaches. We have created the All Saints' Early Childhood Foundation with its own board, separate from the church. The Foundation seeks grants and accepts donations to support music and art instruction for the children, as well as new books for literacy enrichment. We offer literacy instruction for parents, offering child care for their two- and three-year-olds while they attend classes onsite. The Foundation members are advocating within our community for the silent children of poverty and the need for space for quality education programs for them.

Parents are beginning to ask literacy tutors about times for church services and Sunday school. They ask if they may attend All Saints' even after their children are promoted to kindergarten. We are building community. The Foundation offers meals for families during back-to-school and adult education nights. We also support the teachers at the Lockhart Center, by paying for their professional development, substitutes, and materials for classroom instruction.

Over the years, other churches have visited Lockhart, as have our US Senators, our US Representative, and many county leaders. According to Dr. Chris Lowder, Cabarrus County Schools' superintendent, "All Saints' Episcopal Church has created an amazing model for how to make a difference in the lives of children and also how to make a difference in the community. . . . [The Lockhart Early Learning Center] is a beautiful and powerful addition to our community that will change the lives of thirty-six students and their families each year. Even the most cynical among us just might call that a miracle."[38]

Transformation has happened at All Saints'. We suddenly let go of the hard stuff like the lack of money or resources; we fertilized our roots, cut

---

38. Chris Lowder, *Independent Tribune*, "Lockhart Early Learning Center—Community Collaboration at its Best," December 6, 2015, http://www.independenttribune.com/opinion /lockhart-early-learning-center--community-collaboration-at-its-best/article_5d657eac-9c93 -11e5-b926-77ee65bcf001.html

back the dead branches, and we are flourishing as a congregation. God has made the way where there was no way, obstacles were lowered, and more can be done than we think or imagine. We are a self-reliant, self-confident congregation. We love each other; we are a cohesive community of hope. We support each other and our neighbors in the face of violence and tragedy. Only through prayer and the blessings of our Triune God would this be possible. We are on fire with the Spirit.

All Saints' has quietly witnessed to our community. We have opened our doors as a sanctuary, a beacon of hope and light to our silent and most vulnerable children and their families. In becoming active advocates for equity in our public schools, we are reflecting God's love and ensuring care for his creation. As Christians, we must be hope to our children and their families in the public education system. We are Jesus to each other. This is our gospel call: to love one another.

Often as the parishioners reflect on our story, we are drawn to the Nativity Story. Mary, a faithful servant of God, a young Jewish woman, heavy-laden with child, traveling in a foreign land with her betrothed Joseph, had doors shut in her face. "There is no place for you," she was told. Until the innkeeper opened the stable door and gave sanctuary to her and her holy family. All Saints' opened our education wing. We walked in faith, holding tightly to our Lord's hand. Our cup now overflows with blessings, and we will praise our Lord, our God forever and ever. Hope is placed in the heart of a young mother and her beloved children. The All Saints' story is about volunteers being transformed in Christ. Our walk continues every day as we welcome the stranger and walk uncharted paths together.

PART TWO

A Theology of Relationship

CHAPTER FOUR

Public Relationships and Public Institutions

Liz Steinhauser

"Teacher, which commandment in the law is the greatest?" [Jesus] said to him, " 'You shall love the Lord your God with all your heart, and with all your soul, and with all your mind.' This is the greatest and first commandment. And a second is like it: 'You shall love your neighbor as yourself.' "
— Matt. 22:36–39

Relationships with God and our neighbors have been the driving force for all that we do at St. Stephen's Episcopal Church in the South End of Boston. The school partnership that we have been building for the past six years with the Blackstone Innovation School[1] has grown directly from our daily work with young people in our B-READY after-school and B-SAFE summer programs.[2] These year-round academic and enrichment programs serve 175 young people from ages five to twenty-five out of the building of St. Stephen's in the Villa Victoria neighborhood (we serve additional young people in other sites around the city of Boston).

---

1. See http://www.blackstoneinnovationschool.org.
2. See http://www.ssypboston.org/programs.

This *praxis* of providing extended learning programs led directly to our interest and action in building a partnership with the Blackstone School. There is also a *theory*, a theology, behind St. Stephen's school partnership work. This chapter outlines that theology, describes the broader historical context in which we do our education work, and explains the "partnerships of partners" model we use at the Blackstone Innovation School. Our long-term relationships with individual young people—and the adult teachers, parents, and other caregivers who surround them—have motivated us to engage with the public institutions that influence the lives of young people in Boston.

Sin and Separation

In his 1955 book *The Shaking of the Foundations*, Paul Tillich lays out his understanding of sin and grace.[3] As part of his chapter "You Are Accepted," Tillich clarifies that sin is not an immoral act and that there are not "sins" in the plural. Rather, sin is the state of division and separation. We are in a state of sin when we are separated from our true self, when we are separated from our fellow human beings, and when we are separated from God. This state of separation is part of being human and it causes others as well as us to suffer.

But we can lessen the sin of separation. Thanks to grace—being open to God's gift of grace—we can overcome estrangement from each other and God. Grace happens in spite of separation. Grace, according to Tillich, is "the reunion of life with life, the reconciliation of the self with itself. Grace is the acceptance of that which is rejected."[4]

Tillich says "the most irrevocable expression of the separation of life from life today is the attitude of social groups within nations towards each other."[5] In other words, the divisions between people due to differences in class, race, language, ethnicity, geography, age, and other such characteristics is the greatest example of separation and sin.

This seems as true now as it was in 1955. St. Stephen's effort to build a partnership with the Blackstone School is an attempt to follow God's call

---

3. Paul Tillich, *The Shaking of the Foundations* (Eugene: Wipf & Stock, 2012).
4. Ibid., 156.
5. Paul Tillich and F. Forrester Church, *The Essential Tillich* (Chicago: University of Chicago Press 1999), 198.

to be an agent for grace in the world. By building relationships with and between individuals across differences, we are striving to be people engaged in reconciliation and acceptance. By building connections with other people, other lives from whom we have been separated, we take steps toward being reconnected with ourselves and with our God.

Preferential Option for the Poor

Leonardo Boff and Clovodis Boff are just two among a number of Latin American priests and people of faith who defined and described theories of liberation theology. In their 1988 book, *Introducing Liberation Theology*, the Boff brothers outline one of the most basic tenets of liberation theology: a preferential option for the poor and marginalized. Using a range of tools, including scriptural exegesis, Christology, eschatology, and ecclesiology, as well as the model of the apostles' lives and practice, the Boff brothers argue that God in heaven "comes to the help of the oppressed poor." God in Christ makes this preference real with his preaching, healing, and teaching. Christ's law of love, like the Good Samaritan, teaches that we should "approach those who have fallen by the wayside . . . make into neighbors those who are distant, and make neighbors into brothers and sisters."[6] As Christians and leaders in churches we can and should follow this model and instruction for our congregations and ourselves.

By building relationships with young people and families living at and below the poverty line, by investing in public schools that are labeled as underperforming or failing, by supporting students who do not speak English as a first language, by initiating projects in which suburban white adults and youth can build relationships with urban youth of color and their parents, the school partnership work of St. Stephen's Episcopal Church is striving to live out this preferential option for the marginalized.

Tillich Meets the Boff Brothers

What if overcoming the sin of separation required putting those who are marginalized as a priority? What would it mean for grace to have a preferential option for the poor? For me, I usually imagine the best, most healthy

---

6. Leonardo Boff and Clodovis Boff, *Introducing Liberation Theology* (London: Burns & Oates/Seartch Press Ltd, 1987), 44–45.

relationships to be equal in the sense of fifty-fifty sharing. But if Tillich and the Boff brothers (and other liberation theologians) are to hold hands, we need to rethink this relational balance. They would likely say that overcoming the sin of separation and finding the grace of connection does not mean meeting in the middle. Rather, Tillich and the Boffs might suggest that those of us who are privileged (white, wealthy, adults, from safe neighborhoods, beneficiaries of high-quality education) must take more steps toward those of us who are on the margins (people of color, poor, youth, surrounded by risks, students in underperforming public schools). To approach those who have "fallen by the wayside" of society (or, some may argue, who have been pushed to the margins) requires some amount of courage. To make meaningful and authentic relationships with those who are divided from us and to experience the grace of reconnecting with our true selves, our God, and our neighbors, requires real work. More of this work will be and should be the responsibility of those who have had the benefit of living with the privilege and power of our not-yet-just society.

In building the partnership with the Blackstone School, this "extra" effort can be seen in three ways. First, St. Stephen's initiates the partnership with the school. We reach out to teachers, we set meetings with principals, we reset those meetings when they are cancelled, and we wait in school offices when meetings begin late due to an unanticipated student emergency. To create partnerships with urban public schools, in Boston and elsewhere, requires understanding that administrators do not yet see the benefit of such relationships, do not have the time or "bandwidth" to invest much energy in them, and are dubious (based on their past experience) that promises of commitment, good will, and resources will hold true. As a church exploring partnership, it is up to us to make more effort, be more consistent, be more persistent.

Second, St. Stephen's listens to the school. We do not determine for the school what we think is missing or most essential for the school. Rather, we base our partnership work on meeting the needs that are expressed by teachers, administrators, youth, and families. We have built and staffed a library at the Blackstone School in response to teacher meetings as well as research that shows school libraries and library programs are among the most important tools in improving reading ability and reading test scores (a priority for the school). We revitalized the greenhouse and outdoor garden beds at the

Blackstone to support the learning about life sciences, as the standardized test scores showed that 98 percent of fifth grade students were failing or needed improvement to meet the benchmarks in science. We addressed bullying on the school buses to and from another public school, because this was an expressed need from parents and from students who arrived at our after-school program in tears from an upsetting ride.

Third, St. Stephen's is undeterred by obstacles. When the principal changed at the Blackstone for the fourth time in two years, St. Stephen's leaders found ourselves in the position of having to rebuild relationships again from nearly scratch. The shelves of our successfully established library remained under white sheets for months as we struggled with the new administrator to get permission for our same volunteers to be in the building in the new school year. We just kept showing up. When the Edison School and the Boston Public Schools administration disagreed about who held responsibility for funding a salary for a bus attendant (one of the solutions we suggested for curbing bullying on the bus), we aligned ourselves with the school's principal, organized parents, and continued pushing until we received a commitment from the head of transportation to fund the position.

Initiating. Listening. Being undeterred. Taking Tillich and the Boff brothers seriously has meant that the leaders of St. Stephen's have reached past the halfway point as we established the relationships with individual students, administrators, teachers, and parents in the schools. This may not be exactly equal, but it is equitable, just, and necessary, we believe, to increase grace-filled partnerships with public schools. This is the Christian work of building the Kingdom of God in our city.

An Early History of St. Stephen's Church

St. Stephen's has always been a mission church. Established in 1846 by Episcopal City Mission, the congregation's work has had a preferential option for the poor, even before that phrase was coined or popularized. Meal programs, clothing pantries, English language classes for immigrants, kindergartens for young children, and workshops for new parents have been and continue to be part of the ministries offered by St. Stephen's.

For most of our history, this work has been done with an attitude of justice rather than charity. During his travels in America, Alexis de Toqueville cited our first vicar, the Reverend Dr. Eleazer Mather Porter-Wells as one of the people who had done the most to humanize prison conditions and move incarceration from punishment to rehabilitation. Porter-Wells brought this same view of active, justice-filled ministry to his work at St. Stephen's. In the 1890s, the youth work was led by the Reverend Charles Henry Brent, an activist working to build interfaith collaborations against the scourge of opium use, and who later went on to be the first Episcopal bishop of the Philippines. Brent and the laypeople who worked with him at St. Stephen's were part of the settlement house movement of Boston, inspired by Jane Addams and Hull House in their theory and practice of supporting immigrants. While they were not completely able to escape the dangers of noblesse oblige, these early leaders of St. Stephen's understood that the day-to-day work of meeting the immediate needs of the people in the neighborhood around the building of St. Stephen's was directly connected to creating more justice and peace in the broader society. This dual focus continues today.

A History of Boston Public Schools

Parallel to this context of our congregation's history is the history of the Boston Public Schools (BPS). Founded in 1647, BPS is the oldest public school district in the United States. It is a relatively small urban district: in 2015–2016 there were 56,000 students enrolled in 125 schools. Thanks to its size, BPS has been more successful than other cities in addressing some of the challenges that face urban schools. Currently, it has a rising graduation rate (70 percent of students graduate from high school in four years), a measurable commitment to arts education, and improving scores on standardized tests evaluating progress in English language arts and math.

Still, there is a significant gap in the opportunities and education delivered by BPS to students, depending on the particular school and neighborhood, an inequity that is clearly tied to race and class. Like other urban districts, there are rising tensions in Boston as charter schools and regular district schools compete for skilled staff, public recognition, and financial resources. And, quite dramatically, the demographics of BPS (85 percent students of color) do not match the demographics of the city (46 percent people of color); nearly a third of Boston's school-aged children attend a charter, private, parochial, or other school not affiliated with BPS.

All of these challenges are part of the lingering legacy of the 1974 busing crisis that shaped and continues to shape Boston, especially as it relates to public education. Nine years earlier, in 1965, Massachusetts passed the Racial Imbalance Law, which compelled school districts to create schools that were racially integrated. After nearly ten years of the Boston School Committee's refusal to comply with the law, the local NAACP filed a class action lawsuit resulting in a ruling that Boston's schools were unconstitutionally segregated and the imposition mandatory court-ordered busing to integrate the city's schools.[7] Riots in various neighborhoods quickly resulted and made national news; state troopers were posted at the doors of public high schools to protect entering students from thrown rocks and vicious profanity, and innumerable white families relocated to suburban towns and to schools outside the BPS. Within just a few years, BPS lost 30,000 students and the percentage of white students in BPS dropped from 64 to 35 percent. A high level of tension around issues of race defined the city for at least a generation, and even now it is essential that every school policy, news report about BPS, and exchange about public education among parents be seen and understood in the context of this history of institutional racism and its abiding impact.

A More Recent History of St. Stephen's Youth Programs

In 1999, the Reverend Tim Crellin became the vicar of St. Stephen's. He brought with him more than twenty years of experience as a youth worker, much of it in the neighborhood of the Villa Victoria that surrounds St. Stephen's building. What Crellin found was a church in decline in a multiplicity of ways: low attendance, financial confusion, crumbling building, discouraged and divided leadership. He also saw opportunity, both from the long and positive history of the congregation and from the clear needs and interest of the families of the neighborhood. Most members of the community had roots in Puerto Rico or the Dominican Republic, spoke English as a second language, and met the various criteria of living at or below the poverty line. More than half the adults in the neighborhood had not graduated from high

---

7. This period in our city's history is told compellingly in the Pulitzer Prize–winning book by J. Anthony Lukas, *Common Ground: A Turbulent Decade in the Lives of Three American Families* (New York: Random House, 1985). This history is very relevant to our work, as much of the book takes place within five blocks of St. Stephen's.

school. In talking with parents and from his own observations, Crellin could see that the Villa Victoria neighborhood needed youth programming—to meet the immediate day-to-day needs of children and teens—and continued organizing efforts to create more justice on issues of youth programming, economic opportunity, and public education.

Crellin and St. Stephen's leaders were energized by these conversations with neighbors and young people and began to develop a model of positive youth development. Motivated by a gospel call to bring Good News to everyone, especially the poor and marginalized and without regard to participation in Sunday morning worship services, they founded the out-of-school time programs that are now called the St. Stephen's Youth Programs and include the B-READY after-school program and the B-SAFE summer program.

These programs began with twenty elementary school aged children, providing them with a safe place to be during the days and afternoon hours when school was not in session. Nutritious meals, homework help, sports, and some art programming were the essence of the programs in the early days. Over the years, the youth programs have grown in complexity, the age range of the youth served, and the depth of academic support offered. Now, during the school year, St. Stephen's runs B-READY after-school program sites out of two Episcopal churches that are a ten-minute walk apart. The short distance between sites crosses a major thoroughfare, meaning the programs are in significantly different neighborhoods with dramatically different opportunities and challenges. From September to June, we serve 125 elementary schoolers, fifty middle schoolers, and nearly seventy-five teenagers (many of whom have paid jobs as mentors- or counselors-in-training for younger students). In July and August, we add four summer-only sites (also out of Episcopal churches) and run full-day academic and enrichment programming that serves 675 youth across the cities of Boston and Chelsea, including 160 teens, who gain meaningful summer employment.

At each site, with each program, we strive to build communities where all people feel safe, feel big, and feel connected. We believe that long-term, year-round programming—three hundred days a year from age five[8] through twenty-five—is what it takes to transform young people *and*

---

8. Due to current limitations of space, financial, and staffing resources, we start at this age although much research shows the critical importance of interventions that begin even earlier.

transform neighborhoods. We do this by developing the leadership skills of youth and providing the supports and opportunities they need to achieve a healthy and successful life. Then, we work alongside these young leaders as they take action in their own communities. The programs have also provided an opportunity to develop a significant resource: partnerships with more than sixty suburban Episcopal churches that send more than one thousand volunteers to bring food, books, and their care into our B-READY and B-SAFE programs. Thanks to these programs, we have built real, grace-filled relationships among and between staff, volunteers, youth, and families. These relationships have led directly to the adaptations and growth we have made in the programs over the years, including our focus on school partnerships.

As a side effect of these youth programs, the St. Stephen's Sunday morning congregation has been revitalized too. Reflecting a true geographic parish, meaning that we serve a ten-block catchment area around our church building, those who come to worship in our single, bilingual service at 10:30 a.m. on Sunday mornings are about 45 percent Latino/a, 25 percent black (West Indian, African American, and immigrant Africans), 25 percent Anglo, and 5 percent Asian-American. A younger South Korean priest and an older Latino deacon are part of the ministry team. People come together across differences of language, economic class, country of origin, sexual orientation, and theological perspective. Young upwardly mobile white doctors pray, eat, and work alongside Latina grandmothers who live in public housing. It is a remarkable community that continues to grow and fully support the youth programs.

These youth programs are mutual ministry; they are not programs that serve families outside the congregation. There is a clear flow from the Sunday morning congregation to the work in the programs Monday through Friday and back again. While there is no required religious component for youth or staff in the programs, we do offer weekly optional worship experiences that are enthusiastically attended. Consistently, young people and adults report that they see St. Stephen's as their second home and experience the community of friends and mentors as their family; many begin to come six or even seven days a week. (On Saturday mornings, an Ethiopian Orthodox congregation uses St. Stephen's building for worship and fellowship. Some of the young people and teens of that congregation have become a part of the B-SAFE and B-READY programs. On Sunday afternoons, Dignity, a group of LGBTQ Catholics and allies, uses the space for their liturgy; one of the part-time staff people on our Christian education team is from this community.)

Our particular, specific relationships with young people and the families of the Villa Victoria have directly led to the growth and support of the Sunday worshipping congregation, the connections with suburban Episcopal volunteers, and our partnership at the Blackstone Innovation School. We are creating a community—a circle of care around each youth—that is working together to transform young people into leaders and neighborhoods into earthly manifestations of the Kingdom of God.

A Recent History of the Blackstone School

The Blackstone School is directly across the street from St. Stephen's Episcopal Church. It is a school of 630 K-5th grade students, 97 percent of whom are students of color. Half are English language learners and one in five is labeled as having special learning needs. Nearly all of those enrolled meet the various criteria for living at or below the poverty line. While good arguments can be made about the limitations of standardized test scores, they are one tool for measuring the success of a school. The Blackstone's MCAS (Massachusetts Comprehensive Assessment System) scores from 2012 tell an abysmal story. The fifth grade results showed that 85 percent of students failed or needed improvement in math, 87 percent failed or needed improvement in English language arts, and 98 percent failed or needed improvement in science. The school had a long-time principal who was never visible in the building. Parents did not feel welcome and there were almost no family events. Community partnerships were nonexistent. The Blackstone was a prime and unfortunate example of an urban school that served poor students of color and served them poorly, if at all. It was a school that exemplified the sin of separation that comes when our urban school systems do not equitably serve students across differences of neighborhood, race, and class. It was an institution that did not have grace-filled relationships with particular students or parents.

In the spring of 2010, BPS declared the Blackstone to be a Level 4 turn-around school. The long-time principal was forced into retirement, but not before overseeing "irregularities" that resulted in a year's worth of MCAS math scores being thrown out. The school was given three years to meet a variety of goals the state set and defined as demonstrating a successful turn-around. A new principal was brought in, and all the teachers and staff had to reapply for their jobs. A mandate to have 50 percent new teachers actually resulted in 85 percent of the faculty being new. Many of these new teach-ers were experienced and committed teachers who had a vision for turning around the school, using data to drive the classroom teaching and home visits to build relationships with families. The school instituted a new motto—*Ubuntu*—a Xhosa word and concept from South Africa that promotes our interconnectedness and can be translated "we are who we are because of each other."[9] A September 2010 "welcome back" block party with a live band, teachers, and a barbecue brought together more than three hundred people. There was a long way to go to get students and the school to meet the state benchmarks, but with the enthusiasm of the staff and an inspiring vision for the school, it seemed possible. It was—and it truly felt like—a fresh start.

By Thanksgiving break, the energetic and charismatic new principal announced his resignation, lured to Chicago to take an assistant superinten-dent position. By Christmas, he left his post, and for the first two months of 2011, the school was without any principal and was led by an amazing team of administrators. By March, BPS identified a principal willing to come out of retirement to serve temporarily as an interim. Meanwhile, a committee of teachers, parents, and community partners, including a representative from St. Stephen's, engaged in a search process to find a permanent principal. A new leader was selected by a slim majority of the committee, with all the teacher representatives supporting a different candidate.

In September 2011, this new principal, with a three-year commitment signed, began her tenure. A younger woman of color, she had a leadership style that was dramatically different than her white, male predecessor. Rather than encouraging the innovation and creativity of veteran teachers, she was laser-focused on improving the test scores and meeting the benchmarks that would get the Blackstone out of turnaround status. People of good will can disagree about the value of these different approaches; what is clear is that the BPS gave priority to the latter. Teachers initially hired by the innovator-principal bristled at the more rigid, measurement-oriented leadership of the

9. *Ubuntu* has also been developed as a theological concept promoted by Archbishop Desmond Tutu.

new principal. By the end of June 2012, the second year of the turnaround period, half of the newly assembled faculty had left, either by force or choice.

Fall 2012 saw the newest team of faculty working hard with students to build skills in reading, writing, and math. Students were striving to meet new goals and win monthly honors in the Ubuntu values of respect, unity, and excellence. Regular home visits by teachers were expanding the engagement in monthly family events and parent-teacher conferences. Efforts from a committed group of AmeriCorps volunteers from City Year, a program that had been at the Blackstone from the start of the turnaround process, were resulting in more students coming to school each day. By the end of the school year, BPS sent good news: the Blackstone had met all the necessary, state-set goals and could exit turnaround status. What seemed like a great accomplishment worthy of celebration came with the opposite of an award; the school was now expected to maintain this trajectory of improvement without the additional $1 million in annual funding that came with turnaround status. In addition, the principal who had successfully led the school out of the turnaround unexpectedly announced her resignation. For the fifth time in just over three years, the Blackstone would have a new principal.

Fortunately, for the past three years, there has been stable leadership at the Blackstone. Taking a risk on a leader who had never served as a principal but who had the support of teachers, BPS advanced a junior administrator at the school into the role of principal. While this reduced the size of the team of administrators who oversee teacher support and evaluation, curriculum adherence, student attendance and discipline, family engagement and community partnerships, and all other aspects of the school, all four of these dynamic and dedicated women have been with the school since the turnaround process began, thus bringing practical experience and established relationships with students and families to the current "innovation" chapter in the life of the school.

Importance of Context and History

Knowing the history of our city and its institutions—the Boston Public School system, our St. Stephen's Church, and the Blackstone School—have been central to the success of building our church-school partnership. Similarly, understanding the ways federal education policy trickles down to local schools, addressed in other chapters in this book, has been important to our efforts. Recognizing how these broader and historical forces created the local and present circumstances faced by Blackstone students, staff, and families—including the ways that institutional racism influence public education—have helped St. Stephen's in three ways.

First, contextual and historical understanding has helped us recognize the size of the challenges: they are mammoth. The challenges of urban public education did not develop overnight and cannot be solved in a three-year turnaround period. This recognition has encouraged us to build a model of partnership at the Blackstone that is a "partnership of partners." We see ourselves as the convening, rather than sole, organization; St. Stephen's both offers resources directly and recruits other groups that have the resources needed by the school. We understand the project of supporting the school and its students is bigger than we could ever do ourselves.

Second, contextual and historical knowledge encourages us to filter and evaluate our efforts constantly through the lens of larger liberation. Even as we are assembling school supplies for classrooms, we are analyzing the school's budget to understand why these shortages persist. We are asking questions about the city's policy priorities and seeing how these lead directly to inadequate supplies and materials. We are cautious and humble as we experiment and offer solutions, and we can see the ways that seemingly great ideas can be coopted.

For example, in 1993 Massachusetts developed the standardized MCAS test to measure how a newly formulated redistribution of state resources was succeeding in closing the equity gap in and among school districts. This was an admirable purpose. Twenty years later, there is nearly no link to this initial goal. Rather than being a tool for evaluating the policy and districts, the MCAS primarily measures individual students, judging their progress toward state-defined benchmarks in reading, writing, math, and science. The consequences for not doing well on the test are felt by students, often students of color, who cannot receive a high school diploma without passing the exam. The public school administrators and districts do not bear a similar consequence. Understanding how institutional racism and classism influence public policy help us to keep a critical eye on our own efforts, as we strive to be a force for liberation.

Third, contextual and historical reflection helps us stay hope-filled. The work of changing institutions, addressing educational inequity, and supporting students and families who face enormous challenges can be discouraging. Looking back at the past and around at other places offers examples of success and change that can be inspiring. Being part of the All Our Children National Network has been helpful in this way, offering relationships with other people and churches engaged in similar work who can offer stories of struggle and victory that remind us we are part of something bigger. The reflection on the past and broader context helps us have a long view and stay steady in the face of setbacks, such as those that come from building and rebuilding relationships with four principals in two years. We have hope that continuing to show up will indeed make a positive difference for students and families.

Values of our Partnership

Leaders of St. Stephen's are motivated by a theology that emphasizes the building of individual relationships with our neighbors, giving preference to those who are marginalized and poor, as a way to heal from the sin of separation. We are mindful of the contextual forces of history and policy that have created public institutions, including urban public school districts that are inequitable and often disrespectful of the dignity of every human being. We are realistic and humble (or try to be!) about what we can offer to our local school. We initiate and make more than half of the effort to build relationships and make the partnership happen. We strive to listen hard to the needs of the teachers, parents, and students and respond to what we hear, rather than coming in with ideas about what we think the school needs. We expect to encounter obstacles, nearly daily, which helps us to stay steady when setbacks do indeed happen. And we have started small, building on success and keeping a focus on measurable, visible results.

Challenges

Despite all these advances and success, we have encountered a number of clear and ongoing challenges in our partnership with the Blackstone School. Maintaining all the different aspects of the partnership, especially as individuals in key roles change, has been the biggest challenge. So much of our work is relational that as leaders rotate—the school principal, our own partnership organizer, leaders in partner churches—reestablishing those relationships is critical and takes time. After a change in leadership in any one of those roles, we have found that it takes at least three to four months to get back to where we were with a project. Thus, investing in support for the principal (so she stays!) and our partnership organizer staff position (so she stays!) has been a part of effort to overcome this challenge to maintain what we have built.

From the beginning, St. Stephen's saw the work at the Blackstone as a pilot partnership with the hope that we would be able to inspire and support other churches in Boston and the surrounding areas to replicate such a partnership at other schools. Over the past six years, we have made two efforts to replicate, neither of which really got established. One school was quite distant from our site, although many students from this school participated in our summer and after-school programs. We had a great relationship with the principal and hosted a successful kick-off day of action with nearly sixty volunteers, but we were unable to capitalize on the momentum from this event to really establish an ongoing partnership. Efforts to inspire leaders in the Episcopal Church just a half mile from the school never gained traction. Our application to local AmeriCorps programs to gain a person to support the outdoor classroom was rejected. And then the BPS school assignment system changed, so fewer students were shared between St. Stephen's and this school *and* the principal was promoted to a role within the district central office. One lingering success was that the evangelical church that rents the building to use for services on Sunday began to be more engaged in the school on a regular basis.

We also tried to build a partnership with a nearby high school that a number of our teens attend. We established good relationships with key guidance counselors at the school and had a series of meetings with them, along with teachers, administrators, and leaders of other partner organizations in the school, including the ROTC. Unfortunately, the school has some significant challenges with staffing, collaboration, funding, enrollment, and a variety of other basic functions. It made the local papers one year because several weeks into September, class schedules still had not been distributed to students so neither students nor teachers knew where to report or when during the school day. Understandably, staff with whom we had relationships moved on, discouragement among other faculty set in, and another turnaround/transformation plan was designed by the central office of BPS. The challenges at this school, largely related to the institutional racism and systemic poverty that affects all urban schools, seemed too big to overcome, so St. Stephen's leaders turned our attention elsewhere.

Most recently, we have started overcoming this challenge of building a second school partnership by solidifying our work at a school that is five blocks from St. Stephen's. It is a school that is considered a "desirable" choice, with a number of white, middle-class families from the neighborhood enrolling their children, a range of partnerships with local organizations, and an annual gala that raises money for those "extras" that most Boston schools cannot afford. While this has created a school with strong leadership and excellent academics, it has not yet resulted in a cohesive school community. Parent engagement is geared toward the white parent leadership (20 percent of the student body), with meetings held in English only and at times that favor those without full-time employment. Organizing by St. Stephen's parent leaders, who are among the 75 percent of Latino families who attend the school, has led to changes, including shifting meetings to evening times, arranging for Spanish-language translation at all school meetings and events, and getting a number of Latina parents to run for (and get elected to!) formal leadership roles in the school.

A third challenge that we encountered is related to the ongoing decline that is happening within the Episcopal Church, and other mainline Protestant denominations, nationally. US society has changed. Sunday mornings are full of soccer leagues, not a social expectation to attend church. The rise of the "nones" is clear among young adults. Social media has allowed connections and community to happen among people virtually rather than during coffee hour in parish halls. These changes are visible and real in many of the suburban churches with whom we partner. Lay leaders get older and less willing to drive to the city; they are not replaced by younger leaders. The number of people attending Sunday services is lower, resulting in fewer pledging families and smaller budgets for churches. Outreach budgets are smaller; fewer funds are available to support classroom supply drives. In general, a growing number of St. Stephen's partner churches are operating from a posture of scarcity, rather than abundance and generosity. Building a relationship with an under-resourced public school in the city seems like an extra thing that is no longer within the reach of churches that feel they must prioritize their own members' needs and their congregation's survival.

How Are the Blackstone School and St. Stephen's Different Thanks to the Partnership?

Fortunately, this is not what is happening in all our partner churches. And it is not our experience at St. Stephen's. Rather, our experience is that the more we reach out to families in the neighborhood (even if they do not come to worship on Sundays), teens who need employment (even if they have not been baptized or confirmed in the Episcopal Church), and neighborhood schools (even if we do nothing that remotely resembles traditional under-standings of evangelism), the more vibrant and full our church becomes. Our average Sunday morning worshipping community has grown from twenty members to ninety in just over ten years. Our pledging is up 600 percent in that same time period. Teens who have jobs as Counselors-in-Training in our youth programs go on service-learning trips in Appalachia or Honduras and come back with transformed hearts, along with material for college essays. By building a school partnership with the Blackstone School, and investing staff time, programmatic money, and our congregation's spirit into the effort, our church community—and our geographic parish—is healthier. We are living out our gospel call and baptismal promises in the South End.

The Blackstone School is also stronger thanks to the partnership with St. Stephen's. Standardized test scores are up, even though there is a long way to go to get the majority of the student body reading and doing math at grade level. Classes are getting some of the "extras" that regularly happen in other schools, such as art, music, theater, and (of course) library time. As of this writing in the fall of 2016, the administrative leadership team has been in place for more than four years and the teaching staff is mostly stable from year to year. There is a general feeling of teamwork and satisfaction. Daily average student attendance is up, meaning each student has more learning time to advance his or her skills. Family-engagement events happen monthly with more people participating and more community members involved. Students are learning, growing, and advancing their academic skills.

Relationally, the teachers, administrators, families, and students feel sup-ported by an outside organization. While difficult to measure, this connec-tion has helped to create a feeling of importance and being part of a larger community that cares. There is an increase of hope and possibility. We often describe this as a change in the "vibe" of the school. Now when one walks in the door, a visitor sees colorful murals, lively groups in the library, and smiles on the faces of students. This is in dramatic contrast to how it used to be when one walked in the building when there was no feeling of welcome, if one could even find the right door to walk in! Students are proud to wear "Ubuntu" T-shirts with the school logo on them. There is a sense of school pride that was completely absent before.

These changes cannot all be attributed to the church-school partnership, of course. Even the improvement in reading scores cannot exactly be tied to St. Stephen's work in the library, as we don't have any direct research evidence to prove a direct connection. But our efforts to train loving volunteers to support students in classrooms and to infuse the library with clearly cataloged books does seem to be making a positive difference in the school.

Congregants at St. Stephen's and our partner volunteers have built real relationships with students, parents, teachers, and administrators. Our church, our members, the South End community, and our public education system is better for this investment.

CHAPTER FIVE

Partners for the Kingdom

Benjamin P. Campbell

He has told you, O mortal, what is good; and what does the LORD *require of you but to do justice, and to love kindness, and to walk humbly with your God?*
—Micah 6:8

In the fragmented social fabric of early twenty-first-century American cities, partnership between churches and public schools stands out as one of the true signs of hope—both for the schools and for the churches. It is a sign of the Kingdom of God.

Many Episcopal churches are finding that partnering with public schools provides a pathway back into the community. And public schools are finding in the faith community partnerships the support and nurture for children that have been sucked away by society's isolation, deprivation, and secularism.

In the economy of God, we all need each other. Our relationship may appear optional, especially with those privileged with mobility. But it is not. For full life it is essential. The isolation of the society does not just affect the poor. It affects those who are able to function at an economic level that keeps them out of desperation. But many of those, including many Episcopalians, are aware of their own isolation from the needs of others in the society. Because of the inspiration of God's spirit, they are desirous of stitching together the ripped fabric of the community. They are aware that they have material and personal gifts from God, but that their resources mean nothing in isolation. Their resources, often plentiful in both person and goods, are buried in the ground by a culture that isolates them from the community of need.

So we go on mission trips. We give to charity. But nothing really seems to change. The fruits of the effort are brief and temporary, both for us and for the persons whom we endeavor to serve. Meanwhile, the community in which we actually live is still divided; the issues seem to magnify and the great gulfs in community and economy continue to widen.

Partnership between churches and public education is one of the best available opportunities in our time to reopen to both church and the community a comprehensive opportunity for good news and restoration—Jesus's vision of the Kingdom of God.

Churches and schools understand each other as institutions, perhaps better than any others could. Both are community builders; both have a very high volunteer component; both are constantly relating to unpredictable and unplanned situations; both must place individual needs at the top of their priority list; both are continually pastoral in their relationships to their charges; both are dedicated to children, and to families; both place nurture above material wealth; both are concerned with eternal value; both are dedicated to truth; both need a power greater than themselves to restore them to sanity.

Churches are ideal partners for public schools because they are in the business of human nurture, love, and formation for the long haul. Schools are community institutions and will only be successful with strong community support. Both schools and churches are places where the messiness of human relationships is fully displayed. Both are also contexts in which genuine salvation can be witnessed. Relationships are essential to their success. Forgiveness is mandatory. The church that is engaged with a public school is a church that is praying into its relationship with the Kingdom of God. It is not on top of the heap, but a servant of God's healing of the world.

Thus, the evangelism that occurs when a congregation gets involved with a public school goes both ways. The school—teachers, administration, parents, and students—are encouraged and supported, and the resources of the school are enhanced, so that true nurture and opportunity may be endeavored. But the church hears good news as well. Members grow in their understanding of the true glory and beauty of the Kingdom, of the struggle for justice, of the universality of God's intention, and of the power and meaning of the interchange embedded in human community. The Spirit grows, and the Spirit's power spreads throughout the enterprise.

This kind of evangelism is not memory work around Christian formulas and creeds. It is the everyday giving and receiving of good news. Everybody knows, of course, that it is in Christ's name—and it certainly provides an offset to other less salutary things that have received the Christian brand. It also gives a vehicle for the Holy Spirit to draw to the church new persons who have seen the church for the first time as a place where the Spirit of God is active.

Why is the public school so especially important to Christians? Christians had a lot to do with establishing public education in many parts of America, and Christians have a lot to do with sustaining it. For example, black and white church people founded Virginia's public school system and sustained it both when it was racially segregated and when it was integrated. Where public education is dying in America, it is at least partly because Christians have ceased to care. In one particular way, the public school is still the most "Christian" of American institutions. It is Christian because it includes everybody and is based on the principle of God's love for every human being. No other social institution actively lives out that principle. Public education is at great risk because many people do not understand or embrace that task, its difficulties, its costs, and ultimately, its opportunities.

The universality of God's love, regardless of race, religion, gender, income, or any other distinction, is one of the most fundamental of Jesus's teachings. Public schools proclaim that love in practice. Public education is the only institutional context in which Christians can fully live out their support of that principle.

In the public school context, no words of Christian religion are spoken; instead the actual spirit-experience of the Kingdom is lived. The days are about love, nurture, discovery, difference, enlightenment, and sometimes drudging service. Reflection on experiences, both for the maturation and edification of Christian disciples, and for greater understanding and effectiveness of school personnel and students, is an essential part of this relationship. Prayer drives us deeper into service, and that challenging service drives us deeper into prayer.

Engagement with a public school draws new persons into our churches, persons who want to reintegrate the community and serve God effectively. It enlivens the prayer in our congregations. It informs volunteers, school personnel, and parents, and helps to form support for public education and effective nurture of children of all races and income levels.

Engagement of a church with a public school, and on a policy level with public education, gets the church involved not in the periphery of society but in its very center. It is a place where all of the light that the gospel can shine is needed. It proclaims the fundamental inclusiveness, the universality of the gospel. It places human life and nurture back at the top of the American agenda. It refuses to make justice an afterthought, making the prophet an occasional entertainer of the guilty conscience. But it invites full participation in the salvation of the world and the coming of the Kingdom.

Anglicans have several particular strengths in today's American society that give them particular strengths in supporting public education: The Episcopal Church, and the Anglican Communion, are Enlightenment-based in their theology. They believe in education. They understand that true education rather than indoctrination is the best support for faith in God.

Episcopalians are often quite comfortable in interreligious situations, a reality of particular importance in today's public education environment. The multiracial, multiclass reality of public education is central to the commitment of the Episcopal Church. Episcopalians are no strangers to issues of public policy, tax policy, and public support. They are capable of using their influence to advocate for the true needs of public education in our time, as they become informed.

Perhaps the most important benefit of working in public schools for the congregations of Episcopal churches and their members is the opportunity to join in genuine community without the ability to control. The leadership of the public schools, by necessity, controls the schools. Work in the schools is therefore by definition supportive, rather than under the control of the volunteers. Church people who have had the privilege of working in this fashion talk of the relationships with principals, teachers, parents, children, and volunteers from other churches and agencies as a real opportunity for change in their own lives. They come to a broader understanding of other cultures because their own culture may not be in control.

The respectful, nonexecutive, noncontrolling opportunities for service in public schools—often under the leadership of persons from other cultures, classes, or races—have given great gifts of understanding and even of humility to many Episcopalians. This is an essential aspect of the rebuilding of community, and brings a knitting together which firmly supports Kingdom building in our time. One's gifts are made available without control, and the gifts which one receives are also freely given. The mutual respect that is built is a foundation stone for the community that is coming into being. The understanding that comes enables volunteer participants to be of genuine assistance with efforts and resources that are actually needed, rather than some predesigned and convenient gift that satisfies the giver rather than supporting the recipient.

In Richmond, Virginia, much of the experience of churches with public education has come through the development of the Micah Association over the past fifteen years.[10] The Micah Association is an association of 118 faith communities partnering with twenty-three elementary schools in Richmond, Virginia. All but two of the schools have K-5 populations with between 80 percent and 100 percent of the children on free and reduced price lunch. The population of all but one of the schools is more than 95 percent nonwhite. Participating faith communities come from more than fifteen Christian denominations, nondenominational congregations, the Hindu Temple, Jewish synagogues, and the Islamic Center of Virginia.

Micah traces its beginning to a set of hearings held at St. Paul's Episcopal Church in 1998, in which the congregation looked at the needs of the city of Richmond. The goal was to find a single project for ministry and mission to which the congregation could devote significant time and resources. Out of the hearings, it was decided that a partnership should be developed with nearby Woodville Elementary School, which adjoins the Creighton Court Public Housing Project. St. Paul's hired a parishioner to work full-time as the volunteer coordinator at the school, assuring that the volunteer effort would add value rather than take more time from the already severely overburdened staff.

Soon thereafter two other Episcopal churches established partnerships with two other schools adjoining public housing projects in Richmond.

10. See http://micahrva.org.

Meanwhile, the Jewish Coalition for Literacy had established a program at Swansboro Elementary School. The Jewish Coalition and St. Paul's decided to join with Richmond Hill,[11] an ecumenical Christian community and retreat center, to expand the program to more schools and faith communities. St. Paul's agreed that the new organization could take the name Micah Association, since all agreed that Micah 6:8 expressed the commitment on which they were acting: "He has told you, O mortal, what is good; and what does the LORD require of you but to do justice, and to love kindness, and to walk humbly with your God?"

Two individuals volunteered to coordinate the effort between faith communities and schools. Twenty-five faith communities joined. An individual gave a grant for a salary so that a full-time Micah program director could be hired. Richmond Hill donated a nonprofit base, office, and backroom services for the program. Soon there were forty faith communities. Six couples gave five-year pledges for the program director salary. The number of faith communities tripled to 126, with over 1,600 volunteers, and now include twenty-three highly stressed elementary schools in the center city. Today there is still one paid program director with one volunteer assistant.

Richmond Public Schools embraced the Micah Initiative[12] early, perceiving it an essential aid to the tremendous need found in its poverty-concentrated schools. Another partner, Virginia Mentoring Partnership, was essential. That nonprofit organization, with its own funding, has provided training for all the volunteers from the beginning. A second organization, Communities in Schools of Richmond (CIS-R), has grown with the Micah Initiative. CIS-R was just beginning when Micah started at Woodville, and the Woodville coordinator had a joint appointment from both Micah and CIS-R. Today, CIS-R has coordinators in nineteen elementary schools—at least six of the positions having been started with the help of grants from the Micah faith partners. In some schools where there is no CIS coordinator, the school system has designated a staff person to perform that function. In another, a Micah partner has provided a half-time coordinator. In one school, Richmond Hill has historically provided an intern as a half-time volunteer coordinator.

---

11. See http://www.richmondhillva.org.
12. See http://www.richmondhillva.org/serve/micah-initiative/.

In addition, each faith community has a "key coordinator"—a volunteer who recruits people and resources at the faith community and interfaces with the principal and volunteer coordinator at the school. Volunteers are mentors to individual students, classroom assistants, perform special projects, support summer camp programs, sponsor and chaperone field trips, organize Saturday academies, provide supplies, and sponsor tutoring programs. Faith communities seek to meet the expressed need of the elementary school.

The Micah Association coordinates planning and evaluation meetings involving each partner at each school at the beginning and end of each year and holds quarterly city-wide lunch meetings for key coordinators. At the beginning of each year, key coordinators and key volunteers gather at a faith community host for an opening ceremony and training workshops, addresses by the superintendent and a principal, and prayers by the interfaith partners.

The Micah energy has complemented energy from other corporate and individual volunteer sources within the community. The school-based volunteer coordinators broker not only religious and corporate partners into the schools but also other critical social services and nonprofit partners, creating a profile of effective community work in our primary schools. Over the years, the societal conditions that impact the lives of Richmond Public School students and their families persist. This has been compounded by an overall economic downturn and aging school facilities infrastructure.

Micah volunteers have discovered additional ways to support the city schools that extend beyond the walls of the school and the hours of the school day. Some volunteers have begun advocating around the broader issues of increased state funding, grassroots support for facilities improvements, and increasing student and family advocacy efforts. Many volunteers and entire faith communities celebrate students moving on from middle school and high school. Some continue to support students' college careers, investing time and resources as the children they first encountered in elementary school continue to flourish into adulthood.

Essential to the Micah ministry is the prayer of each faith community for its partner school, the children, the faculty, and the volunteers.

Fifteen years after the founding of the Micah Association, eleven churches in the East End of Richmond, in partnership with Bishop Shannon Johnston of the Episcopal Diocese of Virginia, established an unprecedented partnership with Armstrong High School to create a Freshman Academy within the school itself. The churches—Baptist, Methodist, Roman Catholic, Episcopal, and Pentecostal—helped the school hire two additional instructors and a program coordinator to serve a cohort of sixty students who were two or more years below grade level when they entered high school. Without intervention, fewer than half those students would be expected to graduate from high school on time. The churches provided mentors and tutors, special activities, trips, retreats. They found grant monies from foundations, corporations, government agencies, and church bodies. In the first pilot year, this cooperative effort resulted in a 93 percent pass rate in mathematics (compared to 30 percent for their noncohort peers), a 50 percent reduction in absenteeism, a 75 percent reduction in suspensions, and a 1,000 percent increase in parent participation.

Church members, faculty members, administrators, and members of the larger community are excited and hopeful. The program continues as a pilot, and is under study for expansion. The church members intend to show that a school-community partnership, including additional resources effectively applied, can make a significant difference for students in one of Virginia's three most highly stressed urban schools.

The Reverend Sylvester Smith, chair of the Armstrong Priorities Freshman Academy Board, is pastor of Good Shepherd Baptist Church and a professor at nearby Virginia Union School of Theology. "I think if we care about our young people," he said, "we have to be at least as concerned about their graduation from high school as we are about church membership."

CHAPTER SIX

In the Beginning

Catherine Roskam

The pain of racial injustice and division has wracked our church and the many communities where we both proclaim and embody the gospel of Jesus Christ. Our collective prayer and action can begin to heal what is broken and nurture the Beloved Community that is God's dream for all.
—Michael B. Curry and Gay Clark Jennings,
"A Letter on Racial Reconciliation"

It's the summer of 2005. I am standing in a makeshift classroom in a refugee camp in Kibondo, Tanzania. I am impressed with the students and their enthusiasm for learning. The classroom is crowded, though. There are not enough places for the children to sit down, so many of them simply stand or lean on a windowsill. They do not have textbooks or school supplies. It is difficult to get teachers with experience to come to this place.

Three years later, already involved with All Our Children,[1] I am sitting in an auditorium in New York City for a hearing with the Board of Education on changes in school funding. I hear a young middle school

---

1. The All Our Children National Network grew out of the Diocese of New York's All Our Children program described in this chapter.

student from the South Bronx give testimony about his school. The classes are so crowded the students don't all have desks. They have to lean against the walls or sit on the radiators. They have no textbooks and no school supplies. Dedicated teachers often purchase supplies with their own money, but it isn't enough, and it isn't fair. It is difficult to get teachers with experience to come to this place.

The middle school in the South Bronx is an *American* school. How could an *American* school have so much in common with a school in an African refugee camp?

I knew there were inequities among schools in different communities. I had worked in the Head Start program in 1960s New York City, and the Lincoln Center Artist in Residence program in the 1970s, working with children in inner-city public schools.

Yet I was stunned at the extent of this present disparity. The situation had gotten worse, not better, since the turn of the new century.

I am proud to be a product of public education. This was not what I remembered. I remembered excellent teachers and textbooks for everyone, well stocked libraries and science labs, music and art, and in high school a world-class orchestra in which anyone could participate, even if they did not own their own instruments.

I did not grow up in an affluent white enclave. I grew up in a largely middle-class, racially and ethnically diverse town on Long Island. It had a high end and a low end economically, but the high end was mostly professional, not super rich, and the low end struggled to make ends meet a good deal of the time but were not living in devastating poverty. I don't remember the town having a single homeless person.

My high school was integrated. It was the late 1950s. The Supreme Court had already ruled in the case of *Brown v. Board of Education*. Rosa Parks had kept her seat in the front of the bus. My friends and I thought she was right and brave, and that racial discrimination was a Southern problem.

We were still upset about the recent defection of the Brooklyn Dodgers to Los Angeles, taking our hero Jackie Robinson with them.

I thought we were a typical American town.

I was naïve on many counts. I know now my African American friends might have given a different account of those years, if only I had thought to ask.

Still, it was also true that the leaders of the black and white communities were working together behind the scenes through New York's Board of Education for integration and excellence in public education. Surely most towns, at least in the north, were like mine. Surely.

Now I'm not so sure, especially having read Jonathan Kozol's book, *The Shame of the Nation: The Restoration of Apartheid Schooling in America,* published in 2005. It was given to me in 2006 in celebration of my tenth anniversary as a bishop by St. Ann's in the Bronx, a church that does a tremendous amount in the way of supporting public education, tutoring, mentoring, and nurturing the children who attend some of the poorest schools in the state. It is a place where Jonathan Kozol has spent much time with the children of the South Bronx, as his books attest.

The title of the book was a shock, as it surely was intended to be, slicing through our denial about the racial divide in this country, especially as it affects our children. But to me the most compelling call to action within it was Kozol's observation that "the four most segregated states for black students, according to the Civil Rights Project, are New York, Michigan, Illinois, and California. In California and New York, only one black student in seven goes to a predominantly white school."[2]

How could this be? Not one southern state in that list. And two of the worst states, New York and California, were where I had spent all my life! How could I not have noticed?

My husband and I were intentional about sending our daughter to integrated public schools. The polyglot, multiracial environment of lower Manhattan, where she went to primary school, masked the divide that was deepening in pubic schools in other areas of the city.

By the time she was in high school in the early 1990s, we were living in the Bay Area. Caucasians in San Francisco had just become an ethnic group instead of the majority. Our daughter went to a very integrated high school in Marin, which bore more resemblance in its makeup to the integrated high school I attended in the late 1950s than to any of the schools I visited in the mid-2000s in New York.

---

2. Jonathan Kozol, *The Shame of the Nation: The Restoration of Apartheid Schooling in America* (New York: Crown Publishing, 2005), 19.

Even in the 1990s such a school was the exception not the rule, but remembering my own high school and hers, I am reminded that better and more integrated schools are possible if there is a will for transformation. And where better to start than the church?

Like the other New York bishops, I visited the two hundred-plus congregations in our diocese Sunday by Sunday, and I noticed a surprising number of our churches are situated cheek by jowl with public schools. Only a few churches, however, had crossed the parking lot or playground to see how they could be of service. Most of those were inner-city churches, among them St. Ann's, St. Margaret's, San Juan Battista, and St. David's in the Bronx, where the problems of poverty and racial discrimination are part of everyday life. Feeding programs, after-school tutoring and mentoring, advocacy and community organizing had been going on since the 1970s.

But where was the rest of the diocese?

I began to see in the proximity of our churches to public schools a tremendous opportunity to make a difference. I have always believed that when good people have good information, they tend to make positive choices in support of the common good. Even if we are not moved by compassion or altruism, one can make a case, as Alexis de Tocqueville did in *Democracy in America*, published in 1835, for right action as part of enlightened "self-interest rightly understood."[3] That is to say, when we help one another, the quality of our common life is affected positively, and that benefits us as well.

Or as Episcopalians we can see that path as a way to live more fully into our baptismal vows to seek and serve Christ in all persons, loving our neighbors as ourselves, and to strive for justice and peace among all people, respecting the dignity of every human being.

From either perspective, the children of our communities are not only the responsibility of their parents or guardians. They are all our children. That is the reason the initiative we began in support of public education took the name All Our Children.

They are indeed all our children, not only as a society but also as church.

What if every church in the diocese partnered with a local public school? What if every Episcopalian committed time in support of public education?

---

3. Alexis de Tocqueville, *Democracy in America*, 1837, Book II, Section VIII. See http://xroads. virginia.edu/~HYPER/DETOC/ch2_08.htm.

I took the idea first to diocesan Bishop Mark Sisk and then to the Reverend Matt Heyd, chair of the diocesan Social Concerns Committee, and received encouragement and support from both. At that time Matt was on the staff of Trinity Wall Street. He took the idea to Trinity as well, and out of those initial actions was born a partnership between the Episcopal Diocese of New York and Trinity Wall Street for the support of public education.

Support of the All Our Children initiative was embraced in a resolution at our diocesan convention in 2007. Educator Joyce Mondesire, a parishioner of Trinity, and I cochaired the steering committee with oversight of the work that followed.

In the fall of 2008, Trinity and the Diocese of New York cosponsored an All Our Children education conference with Jonathan Kozol as keynote speaker. He was as riveting and inspiring in person as he was in print. Among the other speakers were Don Cowles of St. Paul's, Richmond, Virginia, a mentor with ten years' experience in the Micah Initiative[4]—an education partnership between faith communities and public education, and Dennis Walcott, deputy mayor of New York, who expressed the city's interest in All Our Children.

The audacious goals of All Our Children were these:

1. That every Episcopal Church in the diocese form a partnership with a local public school.
2. That every Episcopalian give forty hours a year in support of public education through tutoring, mentoring, advocacy, or teacher/classroom assistance.
3. That the leadership from these partnerships meet from time to time for mutual support and the sharing of information.

The guidelines for the formation of the partnerships were as follows:

1. That after initial contact was made between church and school, the church would engage in a process of listening to the needs and hopes and dreams for the school expressed by principals, teachers, and children.
2. That the church discern in what ways they had the will and the gifts to help meet those needs and further the hopes and dreams of their partners.

---

4. See chapter 5 for more about the Micah Initiative.

3. That the two move ahead with mutual respect and a clear under-
    standing of expectations and responsibilities.

To be avoided at all costs in this process was for a church to go into a
school with their own preconceived agenda of what they were going to do
without listening first.

The testimony to the faithfulness of the churches in the listening process
was the diversity of programs that ensued. The churches involved were large
and small, affluent and struggling, yet all found productive ways to be of
service in effective and transformative ways.

Grace Church, Monroe, a small church in an area on the cusp between
rural and suburban, began a community garden on their property in partnership with the school. This tiny parish had among its members a number of
experienced and even master gardeners who worked side-by-side with the
teachers and students planting and harvesting, and teaching and learning
in the process. The produce helped to feed the most needy families whose
children attended the school.

Christ Church, Bronxville, a large church in an affluent area, began
an after-school program called "Young at Arts" that brought together the
young people of Bronxville and the nearby poorer communities of Yonkers
and Mount Vernon with professional singers and dancers. Reports abound of
grades going up for the children engaged in this program, despite the long
hours of learning and rehearsal.

In addition to their own tutoring program at a nearby public school,
Trinity Wall Street spearheaded the connection with "Book Buddies," a web-
based program of support for reading, in which former presiding bishop
Katharine Jefferts Schori participated.

Trinity, Mt. Vernon, a black church in a poor area, supported a local
kindergarten with in-class assistance by a group of older women, who also
provided enough person-power so the children had adequate supervision to
go on field trips.

Grace Church, Nyack, generated "The Amazing Grace Circus," whose
amazing performances graced my own retirement celebration (as did "Young
at Arts" and the African drumming group from St. Paul's Spring Valley).

Churches such as St. Ann's in the Bronx and San Andres in South Yonkers continued their indispensable after-school programs, providing mentoring and tutoring and a safe haven away from street life.

The list of participating parishes is too long to include in this essay, but these examples give a sense of the scope of possibilities for diverse churches in diverse contexts. Any church anywhere can do something in support of public education.

That realization took us to the General Convention of 2009, which passed Resolution B025, "Support Equity and Participation in Public Education," delineating our goals for participation across the wider church.[5] A choir performance from "Young at Arts" in the House of Bishops solidified the bishops' support and enthusiasm in initiating the resolution, which passed both houses without debate.

In the first phase of All Our Children, we were grateful for our success in communicating the problem of inequity in public education and offering viable alternatives that would result in tangible and measurable improvement we could celebrate. We also recognized that quite a few other dioceses were involved with public education through different programs, such as the Diocese of Dallas's participation in "One Church, One School."

All Our Children was not intended to be a program but an initiative with certain criteria under which many programs could network. The current iteration of All Our Children, under Lallie Lloyd's leadership, is consonant with that goal and, in its second phase, is energetically and effectively moving All Our Children to a new level.

We are now a decade away from the beginning of All Our Children's first phase. At that time we made a conscious decision to focus on improving public education through advocacy and direct service, engaging only indirectly with underlying issues of racism.

But recent history has opened that conversation for us.

In the last decade we have seen the murder of too many unarmed black men and women. The Black Lives Matter movement brings to the fore racial inequity at every level of our society. Michelle Alexander pulled back the

---

5. Resolution 2009:B025 "Support Equity and Participation in Public Education" http://www.episcopalarchives.org/cgi-bin/acts/acts_resolution-complete.pl?resolution=2009-B025 (accessed February 14, 2017).

curtain on the criminal justice system with her 2010 book, *The New Jim Crow: Mass Incarceration in the Age of Colorblindness* and the effect of the "school-to-prison" pipeline. The privatization of the prison system allows some people to profit off the misery of others without much incentive for prison reform, or reform of our criminal justice system.

Michelle Alexander writes:

> The only country in the world that even comes close to the American rate of incarceration is Russia, and no other country in the world incarcerates such an astonishing percentage of its racial or ethnic minorities. . . . In 1972, fewer than 350,000 people were being held in prisons and jails nationwide, compared with more than 2 million people today. . . . One in three young African American men will serve time in prison if current trends continue, and in some cities more than half of all young adult black men are currently under correctional control—in prison or jail, on probation or parole. Yet mass incarceration tends to be categorized as a criminal justice issue as opposed to a racial justice or civil rights issue (or crisis).[6]

According to the National Center for Education Statistics, it costs taxpayers on average $12,296 per child per year of public school.[7] Governing. com breaks down the latest figures on per capita cost by state, showing the spectrum between the lowest, Idaho at $6,621, and the highest, New York at $20,610.[8] But even those averages can be deceptive, as within states minority schools often get a much smaller piece of the pie, while schools in white affluent areas, drawing on higher property taxes, have much more money to spend.

By contrast, it costs taxpayers on average $31,286 a year to keep a person in prison, ranging from $14,603 in Kentucky to $60,076 in New York.[9]

6. Michelle Alexander, *The New Jim Crow: Mass Incarceration in the Age of Colorblindness* (New York: New Press, 2010), 8–9.

7. NCES.ed.gov, figures apply to enrollment numbers for 2014–2015 academic year.

8. Governing.com bases its calculations of per pupil cost on current spending data published in US Census Bureau Annual Survey of School Systems.

9. Christian Henrichson and Ruth Delaney, *The Price of Prisons: What Incarceration Costs Taxpayers* (New York: Vera Institute of Justice, 2012), based on a survey of forty out of fifty states. See http://archive.vera.org/sites/default/files/resources/downloads/price-of-prisons-updated -version-021914.pdf.

The cost per inmate for New York City jails tops the charts at a staggering $167,731.[10] Even by de Tocqueville's "enlightened self-interest," mass incarceration is insupportable. It serves no purpose other than the nefarious twins of greed and racism that undermine our society as a whole.

How much more egregious are these facts then, when we followers of Jesus apply the template of serving Christ in all persons, loving our neighbors as ourselves, working for justice and peace, and respecting the dignity of every human being? Prison reform is imperative. Reform of our criminal justice system is also imperative. Restoring education to prison inmates is crucial.

And while this is going on, what about the children in our public schools now? Those of us involved in All Our Children are committed to addressing the now and the near by helping to improve public education for all our children, not just the affluent ones, by getting involved in local schools as tutors and classroom volunteers, by becoming advocates for more equitable funding at city and state levels, by supporting restorative justice in discipline to help stem the tide of young black and Latino youth lost to incarceration every year, and by making excellence in public education viable for all.

Presiding Bishop Michael B. Curry has called us as Episcopalians and Christians to focus on reconciliation, and on racial reconciliation in particular. Public education is a rich arena for such endeavors.

History has already taught us that separate is not equal. We can move toward a more just society, toward greater equality and opportunity of all our children today by taking that first step across the parking lot or across a neighborhood to offer to be of service to a school whose cultural and racial makeup is different from our own. This can pave the way for fuller integration over time, an integration that does not subsume one culture into another, but lives together with the full agency and mutual respect the gospel requires.

May God in Christ give us the will to do such things and the strength and perseverance to accomplish them.

---

10. Marc Santora, "City's Annual Cost per Inmate $168,000, Study Finds," *New York Times*, August 23, 2013, http://www.nytimes.com/2013/08/24/nyregion/citys-annual-cost-per-inmate -is-nearly-168000-study-says.html. The article cites a study by Independent Budget Office.

CHAPTER SEVEN

Turnaround

Audrey Henderson

Michael was suspended yesterday
missed the lesson
didn't learn the word refined—
of oil or sugar
but he knows the word restrained.

I know the word restrained.

His school is in receivership, in turnaround,
a failing school,
three years, three separate principals,
stars and stripes
whipping the flagpole, frayed.

CHAPTER EIGHT

An Ecumenical Public Education Initiative

W. Andrew Waldo

As shepherds of our churches, we are charged to lead the faithful in ways that direct our energies to the building up of the Kingdom of God and to make a difference around us. We believe that Jesus' desire for the unity of his followers (John 17:20–23) calls us to work together, and we are conscious as well that "no one should seek his own advantage, but that of his neighbor" (1 Corinthians 10:24).

—Statement on Public Education from LARCUM

Until 2012, when five new South Carolina bishops began to become action-oriented, our history had not borne much in the way missional fruit. We were Herman Yoos, of the Evangelical Church in America, Andrew Waldo and Charles von Rosenberg of the Episcopal Church, Jonathan Holston of the United Methodist Church, and Robert Guglielmone of the Roman Catholic Diocese, and we had followed the example of our predecessors. Every year we participated in a fall theological dialogue and ecumenical service held during the Week of Prayer for Christian Unity. We had embraced that structure from our past, as well as the intention to be one in Christ. As each theological dialogue or service concluded, we'd give thanks for our relationship in Christ and return to our busy, almost tribal, silos, only to gather again later to plan the next dialogue, or the next service. While each of our worlds engaged the world beyond ourselves, we had not yet imagined how to engage it *together*.

This changed in 2012 when a new immigration law came into effect in South Carolina. Its lack of compassion and harsh deportation provisions—including no opportunity for an undocumented person in custody to call his or her family—got our attention. In the midst of this unfolding injustice, we planned our fall dialogue. As our keynote speaker laid out the biblical notions of hospitality and refuge for the sojourner in the land, we realized things were out of balance. Most of us already knew this theology well. Most were also itching to do something compassionate and concrete on behalf of undocumented persons in South Carolina. Out of that sense of urgency we were to form plans for action, as well as to build friendship amongst one another.

We agreed to pray in front of the federal courthouse on the day the challenge to the new law was being heard. Simultaneously, our Lutheran brothers and sisters negotiated an agreement with the Richland County sheriff in the Columbia area to test a pilot ID project in which they created laminated photo IDs for undocumented persons, naming local church contacts on each ID. Any undocumented person who was taken into custody with such an ID would be allowed to call that church contact (often a lawyer-parishioner) and be given a chance to notify family members of their situation.

Thankfully the federal court in Charleston rejected the harshest provisions of the law, rendering those IDs unnecessary. We bishops, however, began to sense a call from God with a new imagination and collaborative authority for action on behalf of the truly powerless in our state.

Immigration injustices had changed our orientation from a talking group to a group focused on action. Earlier in 2012, we had begun conversations about our frustrations with inequities in the funding of South Carolina's public schools and wondered what sort of role we might play in challenging those inequities. As a result, we South Carolina bishops from the Lutheran, Anglican (Episcopal), Roman Catholic, and United Methodist denominations (LARCUM) found a united voice for justice and a plan of action on behalf of our state's most impoverished and powerless people.

The Bishops and South Carolina Public Education

Profound inequities in the South Carolina public education system had been brought into public view through a 2006 documentary film, *Corridor of Shame*, produced and directed by Bud Ferillo, a South Carolina native.[11] This film documented evidence presented in support of eight representative plaintiff districts in *Abbeville County School District v. The State of South Carolina*, a complaint first filed in November 1993. That complaint charged the State of South Carolina with failing to meet even its low constitutional requirement to provide "a minimally adequate education to all its citizens." Thirty-six school districts eventually joined the suit as plaintiffs. The documentary focused its evidentiary lens on schools along South Carolina's I-95 corridor.

A December 2005 state ruling in the case held that, with the exception of early childhood education, the State *did* meet its constitutional standard to provide "a minimally adequate education." Other districts joined the suit, and together, the plaintiff districts voted in 2007 to appeal that ruling to the South Carolina Supreme Court, with final arguments occurring in June 2008.

In 2011, early in her first term, Governor Nikki Haley called upon the churches to "do more" in support of public education. She did not specify what that "more" might be. Hearing her call, many faith leaders at first felt despair, recognizing that we were and are incapable of providing meaningful salary support for teachers, maintenance of school buildings, effective transportation for students, or sufficient school supplies or food for all of South Carolina's needy children. Furthermore, the racial bias underlying our state's educational inequities was obvious: the vast majority of children who were short-changed by these inequities were African American.

So in early 2012, when we bishops identified the urgent and life-denying reality facing tens of thousands of South Carolina school children, we found an issue on which, jointly, we could have a significant impact. While it makes a difference when our churches collect school supplies, backpack lunches, uniforms, and other items of support, most importantly all impoverished children need tutoring, mentoring, after-school enrichment, summer camp, and

---

11. See *Corridor of Shame*, dir. Bud Ferillo, Ferillo & Associates, 2006, http://www.corridorof shame.com.

exposure to the arts *in relationship with committed adults in safe environments over a long period of time.* We had to work to discern what the churches *could* do. We knew that the impact of public statements on an issue was directly proportional to the real commitment of our own constituencies to this issue.

Among the many private and public South Carolina organizations and institutions that have been working to support public education, the Riley Institute at Furman University—led by former South Carolina governor and former United States secretary of education, Richard Riley—has played an especially substantive, persistent, and constructive role in many key areas.[12] In the spring of 2013, the bishops of the South Carolina Bishops' Initiative on Public Education ("the Initiative")[13] met with former Governor Riley and members of his staff to begin discerning how we, as followers of Jesus Christ and South Carolina judicatory leaders, could most effectively advocate for our children.

In 2014 Dr. Tammy Pawloski, director of the Center of Excellence to Prepare Teachers of Children of Poverty at Francis Marion University in Florence, South Carolina,[14] delivered the keynote address for our annual Bishops' Dialogue. Dr. Pawloski's work responds to research about the effects of poverty on brain development. Her ability to translate scientific research into concrete stories and passionate language instantly conveys both the urgency and the basis for hope for these children into pragmatic strategies for teachers of impoverished children. Dr. Pawloski deeply captured our imaginations. Like Governor Riley, Dr. Pawloski has become a key ally in helping us to turn "why" into "how" and "what."

As bishops, we represent about 1,600 congregations and more than 500,000 church members. Before acting, we needed to discover what our congregations were already doing. So the Episcopal Diocese of Upper South Carolina created a survey to answer that question that was first used by our own congregations and then modified for use by the other judicatories. At this initial stage, with relatively little publicity about our intentions, we were glad to get a 20 to 25 percent response rate. The survey uncovered widespread congregational emphases (across judicatories) on programs that provide food

---

12. See https://riley.furman.edu/.
13. See www.bishopseducation.com.
14. See http://www.fmucenterofexcellence.org/.

and supplies to public school children, and a significant number were also engaged in tutoring and after-school enrichment programs. Too many congregations had no connection at all.

A path forward emerged: we would begin by rallying parishioners across our judicatories to serve as tutors and mentors to fill gaps in school districts large and small; urban, small town, and rural. Our loosely organized Initiative could not supply or administer the opportunities to serve, but we could encourage even the smallest congregations to connect with nearby schools or districts or other education programs. It has been remarkable to discover how many public school teachers, principals, and superintendents have emerged from within congregations to structure the Initiative at local levels. In other words, this Initiative is truly being organized, populated, and lived out from the ground up.

By April 2014, we were ready to speak out, so we published a joint pastoral letter to the Lutheran, Episcopal, Roman Catholic and United Methodist people of South Carolina that outlined our intentions.[15] A joint statement from these diverse, though related, religious traditions and perspectives was a striking new element in the public conversation. It signaled our long-term commitment to the members of our churches, public education advocates, Governor Nikki Haley, and our legislators.

Getting parishioners broadly involved means forming new relationships, communicating needs, and above all, remembering that discerning, acknowledging, and developing the God-given gifts in every child has been the work of the Church for centuries and is at the center of God's mission in creation. Doing this work in the United States, with constitutional boundaries between church and state, presents a significant relational and structural challenge.

As noted, the churches we shepherd began organizing at the congregational level. In weekly visits and special conferences, in conventions and liturgies, we have urged parishioners to make long-term commitments to underserved children in local schools as tutors and mentors. Those already doing this have served as witnesses to their neighbors and peers, conveying the power and depth of impact of this work.

---

15. See http://bishopseducation.com/about/bishops-statement-on-public-education/ (accessed October 18, 2016).

I especially remember presenting the Bishops' Initiative to the vestry at St. Thaddeus Episcopal Church in Aiken, South Carolina, in 2014. Few if any of the vestry members had heard of it. As I described our hopes for enlisting parishioners to this holy work, one woman's eyes kept brightening, and she looked as if she would burst with excitement.

She said, "I've been tutoring a little boy for the past four years, since he was six years old. I've clearly made a difference in his life, but he has *transformed* my life!" She paused before adding, "But I've been doing it through Rotary International. . . . Is that okay?" I smiled.

Our invitation is for people to engage whatever local programs most effectively raise up children who are literate and curious in their learning. Our prayer is for all our children to experience "the gift of joy and wonder in all [God's] works,"[16] through whatever programs reach them.

Day-to-day oversight of making connections and enlisting volunteers required that the Initiative hire a coordinator. After developing specific goals, funding streams from each judicatory and a job description, we hired the Reverend Susan Blackburn Heath, an Episcopal priest with statewide connections, passion, and skill for this work. Supervised by the Episcopal bishop of Upper South Carolina, Heath reports on developments and shared work to the assembled ecumenical bishops at regular meetings. Several key components of this initiative have emerged in our work together:

- Norms and standards for engaging schools include a strict nonproselytizing policy and urge volunteers to make two- to four-year commitments to children or their school.
- A focus on developing relationships of trust with district superintendents, principals, teachers, and parents reinforces our focus on the children and their families, not on religious agendas.
- The development of two pilot initiatives: Camp AIR ("Adventures In Reading"), a two-session week-long summer camp for children from Richland County School District One and Aiken County School District; and "Reading Matters," an even wider interfaith recruitment

---

16. From the prayer over a candidate at Holy Baptism, Book of Common Prayer (New York: Church Publishing, 1979), 308.

and training program for tutors in Richland County School District One. Now in its second year, "Reading Matters" includes tutors from the following religious traditions:

- Lutheran
- Episcopal
- Roman Catholic
- United Methodist
- Pentecostal Holiness
- Christian Methodist Episcopal
- African Methodist Episcopal
- Presbyterian
- Southern Baptist
- Columbia Metro Baptist
- Anglican (ACNA)
- Refuge Temple Church
- A house church
- The Downtown Church
- Jewish Reformed
- Islamic
- "Nones"

Moving Forward

On November 12, 2014, the South Carolina Supreme Court ruled in favor of the plaintiff districts in *Abbeville v. South Carolina*. In its ruling, the Court charged the General Assembly to resolve the inequity in funding South Carolina public schools and to address several specific needs in so doing.

In 2015, Jay Lucas, Speaker of the South Carolina House, formed the Task Force on Education Policy Review and Reform and charged it with developing a comprehensive response to the *Abbeville* ruling. This task force requested Initiative bishops to testify at its public hearings. We were the only people to testify who were not professional educators or directly connected to the trial.

The Bishops' Initiative has had an important role in the legislative process affecting public education. Molly Spearman took office as South Carolina's new state superintendent of education in January 2015. We knew the Initiative was gaining traction when both Superintendent Spearman's office and the chair of the House Task Force on Education Policy Review and Reform asked to meet with the Initiative's bishops. During a January 2015 meeting with Superintendent Spearman (her moving boxes weren't yet unpacked), we discovered we shared a vision for the children of South Carolina. We assured her that our commitment is to the children and not to religious or proselytizing agendas. Her own passion for South Carolina's poorest children was evident and encouraging. Spearman had taught in both the poorest and the wealthiest school districts in South Carolina herself. She has since been a keynote speaker at our October 2015 South Carolina Bishops' Dialogue on Public Education, engaging with us and the many parishioners, teachers, volunteers, clergy, school board members, and principals who have begun attending that event since the Initiative was set in motion.

The South Carolina Senate Education Committee began its work in late fall 2015 and requested only two testimonials at its initial hearing: the first by Superintendent Spearman and Michael Brenan, chair of the South Carolina Board of Education; the second by Bishops Waldo and Yoos from the Initiative. At the end of our testimony, Senator John Courson, committee chair, invited the bishops to submit their three most critical agenda items for the legislative reform to the committee. One of them, an increase in teacher salaries, which had been on the agenda of many advocacy organizations and agencies, has already been addressed as of this writing. Not all teachers received a raise; what passed were increases for teachers in rural districts, which created an incentive for teachers to go and to stay in these challenged areas.

In the meantime, Initiative bishops have begun deepening our relationships with legislators of faith through an annual bipartisan breakfast at which we pray, reflect on Scripture, and discuss moral and legislative issues related to the Initiative. We all find motivation and inspiration for this work in God's call to us in Christ Jesus on behalf of the children of South Carolina, and we all explicitly affirm our commitment that our work in the schools be focused entirely on the children whom we are serving—acting, loving, and serving as Jesus would, without pontificating.

We are gaining insight from our new and evolving relationships.

Many of our parishioners have discovered life in new relationships with children in whose lives they can make an extraordinary difference. Teachers are finding new hope in the support and friendships that develop when an adult embodies a community of care by showing up and helping a struggling student. Congregations enjoy new energy and focus in common mission not only within their own traditions, but ecumenically and in interfaith relationships. Legislators appreciate and respond to collaborative, positive, and nonpartisan leadership from the community and the willingness of those community leaders to provide moral cover and support for risky and courageous political decisions. They also recognize that thousands of their constituents are deeply informed by their personal relationships with children of poverty and now know firsthand how funding inequities directly and negatively affect young minds and lives.

These informed constituents ask their representatives questions, and follow legislation and votes. Some are willing to pay higher taxes to fix the state roads and use the surplus for salary increases, improved facilities, and curriculum, and they are making their message heard. Knowledge of and experience with our community members leads to change.

Our commitment is long-term, and for the foreseeable future we have laid aside other ecumenical work to focus on change in public education. While religious advocates for public education have deeper challenges in other regions of the country, we are profoundly aware that the Southern culture's inherent respect for religious leadership is a gift to this Initiative. Setting clear norms, accountabilities, and firm boundaries to avoid religious proselytizing helps cultivate and maintain the environment of trust necessary for this work. We have developed trust that will lead to deeper relationships that we hope will in the future effect more positive change in areas such as racial reconciliation.

Awareness of our Initiative continues to grow, and churches and parishioners continue to ask how they can get involved. We are in the process of reissuing the 2013 public education survey to all of the parishes in our judicatories. We will learn how they are partnering with schools. The number of participating judicatories and congregations is also growing. We are in active conversation with African Methodist Episcopal, African Methodist Episcopal Zion, and Christian Methodist Episcopal leadership about officially expanding the Initiative, an expansion that would then potentially encompass more than 800,000 South Carolinians.[17] The potential of that level of engagement, collaboration, and relationship building among religious entities in common mission in service of our communities is limitless.

This chapter just skims the surface of the many collaborative efforts going on with like-minded civic organizations—statewide, regional, and local—with whom we are in contact. Our work together fills us with gratitude for the Spirit flowing through churches and communities across the state on behalf of all our children.

---

17. On October 12, 2016, the annual South Carolina Bishops' Dialogue on Public Education conference was held at Trinity Cathedral in Columbia. At this gathering it was announced that LARCUM will henceforth be known as The Fellowship of South Carolina Bishops. As of this writing, it includes the African Methodist Episcopal, Roman Catholic, United Methodist, Episcopal, and Evangelical Lutheran Churches of America churches. The SC Bishops' Public Education Initiative is a joint project of the Fellowship. See http://bishopseducation.com/2016 -bishops-dialogue-a-success/ (accessed October 18, 2016).

PART FOUR

The Reality of Socioeconomics

CHAPTER NINE

Gaps and Crosses

A. Robert Hirschfield

Growing up is about learning from mistakes, but the mistakes are relatively costless for affluent kids and often derail poorer kids from the path of success.
—Robert D. Putnam, *Our Kids*

They are called scissor graphs: depictions of the widening disparities that are already tearing apart the fabric of our society. In one graph, for instance, a line moves upward on an axis that shows the amount of time parents of a certain range of income might spend reading *Goodnight Moon* to their child at night. On the same graph, another line shows how few hours are spent reading to a child by parents who are bumping along at the poverty level. The wealthier the family, the more likely the parents will spend time reading to their child. Conversely, the less income a family has, the less likely parents will read to their kids. Another graph may show how high schools in high poverty areas, where at least half the student population qualifies for free or reduced lunch subsidies, tend to offer fewer Advanced Placement courses than in towns where property values, and their tax bases, are higher. The widening space in between these two lines of data has been called the "opportunity gap."

I was introduced to the idea of a scissor graph by reading the Harvard sociologist Robert D. Putnam's groundbreaking book *Our Kids: The American Dream in Crisis* (Simon & Schuster, 2015). It was at a meeting convened by philanthropic, academic, business, and political leaders in New Hampshire who were hoping to bring the topic of these widening gaps to the attention of the dozen or so political candidates who were about to descend on the Granite State in advance of the 2015 presidential primary, always among the first in the nation.

It was not long before I had to confront the uncomfortable truths of the scissor graphs of my own life and of my work as a bishop in the Episcopal Church. That position requires me to sit on the boards of trustees of two private boarding schools in New Hampshire. Both of these secondary schools, the Holderness School and The White Mountain School, were founded by, and continue to be affiliated with, the Episcopal Diocese of New Hampshire. The bishop of the diocese, as part of the bylaws on file in the state's attorney general's office, is the president, ex officio, of the schools' governing boards. In other words, the relationship with the Church is part of each school's constitution and reason for being. Bishop William Niles founded each school in the post–Civil War era when many private schools began appearing on the American educational landscape. Presumably, the public school movement was still in its early stages in the United States, and yet the families of the emerging middle class of the industrializing society recognized that quality education was essential if their offspring were to participate in the benefits of the growing economy. If they wanted their sons (always their sons) to be captains of industry and commerce, leaders of society and politics, a quality education was deemed mandatory, as much for the social networks that were solidified in these schools as the intellectual knowledge that was conveyed in the classroom. A similar principle was in play for their daughters: proper schooling was proper.

Bishop Niles, witnessing how boys of wealthy families from New York and Boston were arriving at the newly established St. Paul's School in the Millville section of Concord, decided that he needed to address the needs of boys and girls of more modest means. As a result, he founded the Holderness School for boys in 1879 in the southern foothills of the White Mountains and St. Mary's School for girls in Concord in 1886. In the 1930s, St. Mary's moved to the more rural setting of Bethlehem, New Hampshire, after a patron donated a sizeable tract of farmland with mountain views. When St. Mary's School decided to admit boys in the early 1970s, it changed its name to the White Mountain School. Over the course of roughly the last half century, the link between the Church and these schools has varied in emphasis, depending on the attention of the bishops and the tolerance of the board to embrace religious affiliation.

Currently, the cost of attending each of these schools comes close to $60,000 a year. Each school reports that the actual cost is somewhat more, and the margin between that and what a family pays is made up by endowment funds that support both financial aid and the general operating expenses of the schools. In addition, some families will pay several thousand dollars more than the base tuition and expenses to cover supplemental academic support in the form of individual tutoring or mentoring so their child will not fall behind in their areas of study. A consultant in independent school organizations informed one meeting of the board that the cost of private school education could easily rise to $100,000 per annum per student over the next decade.

In contrast, state-wide statistics about public education in New Hampshire show per student per year expenditures as low as about $10,000 in towns like Rochester and Manchester, towns with higher rates of children who qualify for free or reduced lunch. Towns like Hopkinton or Bow, where residents pay more taxes based on higher property values, spend on average $18,000 per student.

As the scissors widen, the Church is called to speak to the gaping disparities in how children are raised and educated. Personally, the splaying is increasingly uncomfortable, especially when I consider the benefits I gleaned from attending a prestigious New England boarding school in the late 1970s. Back then, a Choate Rosemary Hall education was not out of reach for my father, who earned a comfortable but not extravagant middle-class income as a tableware salesman. The school provided sufficient tuition scholarship to allow me to attend. It took some convincing for my parents to agree to my attending a prep school and to override their suspicions and apprehensions about my entering a culture that was mostly foreign to their modest backgrounds. My parents were the first in their families to attend college: my father with the help of an ROTC stipend, and my mother with the help of scholarships at a state teachers' college that made her the first in her family to leave the family farm.

Variations in School Funding A

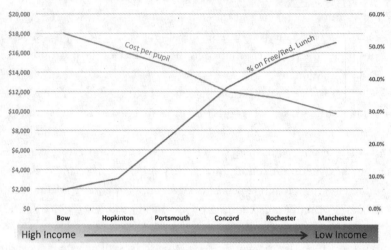

Source: NH Department of Education, Cost per pupil by district 2012-2013.
Kids Count, Children eligible for free and reduced lunch, 2013.

Variations in School Funding B

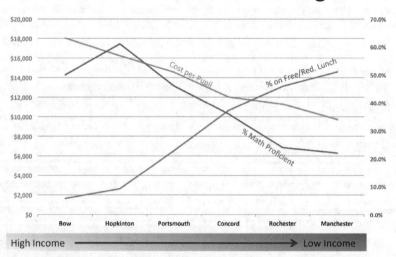

Source: NH Department of Education, Cost per pupil by district 2012-2013.
Kids Count, Children eligible for free and reduced lunch, 2013.
NH Department of Education, High School NECAP Results, 2013.

A debilitating physical injury led to a series of disruptions in my academic and social development in my early teen years. It was partly through the recommendation of our local Episcopal parish priest that I was introduced to Choate, located in the neighboring town. There was no discussion about any ideological commitment to public school education: as I recall my parents did not debate the pros or cons of public versus private education and our loyalty to local public high school. We just did what seemed advantageous at the time. Because we had sufficient resources and the support of the private school offering my admission, we were able to make a choice. We were privileged, and that privilege, I must now own, was only enhanced as a result of that choice. It has led, over time and a series of decisions and advantages, to my now serving as president, albeit ex officio, of the boards of two schools that share, to a greater or lesser degree, a similar heritage as my alma mater. My school saved my life at a time of deep emotional turbulence, as I hope any school with healthy, caring relationships between students and faculty and coaches might enhance the lives of the youth it serves. But there are more hidden costs to these blessings, separate from the price of tuition and room and board, that I now see are accruing to all of us, as the children of our society are increasingly divided.

In the diocese I serve, there are many public schools where the faculty are stretched so thin that such healthy relationships are simply impossible. Some schools in New Hampshire can no longer offer extracurricular activities due to very limited budgets that seem tighter every year. Music lessons, intramural athletics, dance, and tutoring all require a family to pay an extra fee, sometimes hundreds of dollars per semester, prohibiting children who cannot even afford lunch from participating. The New Hampshire legislature's strong resistance to an income or sales tax—candidates for elected public office are pressured to "take the pledge" against such taxes as a litmus test of their worthiness to run—means that property-rich towns offer substantially more opportunities for young students than nearby property-poor towns.

As Robert Putman also notes, parents in these wealthier communities are much more likely to attend churches, synagogues, mosques, or other spiritual assemblies, and bring their children, than in poorer communities.[1] I find it noteworthy that private school administrators hear very few complaints from parents of children at the Holderness School that their child is required to attend weekly chapel, which often includes the Holy Eucharist. Presumably, non-Christian parents either do not object or acquiesce to this practice if it allows their child to benefit from the advantages of a private school education.

As I sit on the board of these private schools as their bishop, I am simultaneously being made increasingly aware of the inequalities of educational opportunities available to children right down the road, even within the same townships and communities where these schools are located, though bordered by well-maintained playing fields and lawns. That awareness impels me to renew the Church's commitment to the New Hampshire children and youth who do not have access to state of the art academic buildings dedicated to STEM (Science, Technology, Engineering, and Math), hockey rinks, dedicated art buildings, or even ski slopes designed by an Olympic development team. One might ask, as I have asked myself, does a bishop of the Church belong on such a board, if it serves to only perpetuate and widen the inequalities in our educational landscape?

The founding impulse of these schools to educate children of more modest means seems to have long since expired, as children of families of ample means ("full-pay families" is the term) are given preference in order to provide the resources needed to keep schools competitive with their peers. Simultaneously, as the founding rationale no longer has much currency, the schools find themselves asking, what is the value and the purpose of maintaining their "Episcopal identity"? If those discussions lead our schools to deeper practices of curiosity, compassion, and courage in addressing the colossal environmental, social, religious, and economic challenges that face us, then count me in. If, on the other hand, retaining their Episcopal Church affiliation is mere window dressing to make the schools more attractive to a segment of our society that still identifies our denomination with privilege and advantage over the unprivileged and disadvantaged, then I will need to vote to secede.

---

1. Robert D. Putnam, *Our Kids: The American Dream in Crisis* (New York: Simon & Schuster, 2015), 4, 10, 89–90, 193, 201, 259.

Increasingly, I see my presence on the boards and my participation in the biennial gatherings of the National Association of Episcopal Schools as an act of obedience to the vows I took at my ordination to the priesthood to love and serve the people among whom I work, caring alike for "young and old, strong and weak, rich and poor."[2] These vows, and those taken at my episcopal ordination to "stir up the conscience of the people," impel me, and by extension the Diocese of New Hampshire, to commit to addressing the opportunity gap that is widening among the youth in the Granite State.

I take it as evidence of the Holy Spirit at work among the churches in New Hampshire that almost every parish has already been moved to address the needs of children and youth. From the northern tip of the state where over 50 percent of children qualify for free and reduced lunch, as the timber and paper industry has almost completely vanished and the local economy struggles to be reconfigured, to the south where many families have access to jobs in the robust high-tech, bio-medical, and defense industry, almost all the churches in our diocese are taking entrepreneurial initiatives to enhance the lives of children.

When the leadership of a church in Concord established a "Take-a-Tot" program to close the gap in nourishment for children who are fed in school but not adequately during the weekend, they became known in the neighborhood as "the church that feeds kids." In the wide range of tags the Church bears these days, that's one we can welcome. All studies show that children are more alert and prepared for learning when they are not hungry.

Another church initiated an after-school choir program where elementary and middle school youth are offered mentoring and homework tutoring in addition to learning how to sing together. Since the choir sings on Sunday morning, the children are required to attend church in order to share their developing musical competencies. Not insignificant is the opportunity for adult members of the congregation to engage in conversations with children and their families who would not otherwise come to church. If we take Jesus at his word, it's more likely that the gospel will be shared from the child to the adult than the other way around.

I know that is the direction of God's evangelism in yet another church, also located in a once thriving mill town now besieged by the opioid

---

2. Book of Common Prayer, 531.

epidemic. Adults show up before dawn in the cold winter to open the doors of their heated undercroft so that children can wait in warmth and safety and have a warm breakfast after their guardians (not always their birth parents) drop them off on their way to work before the school building opens. If the Church did not know how it was called to pursue God's mission before it was made aware of these students' deep need and this opportunity to see the face of Jesus in a hungry and cold child, it does now.

On one point of the scissor graph is a child whose only exposure to cold is in a newly constructed hockey rink, on a ski slope, or in the woods during an Outward Bound–type adventure that is part of the pedagogical tradition of her prep school. On another point is the child who sits under the glaring fluorescent light of a church basement in the early morning before her school has opened its doors. In between these points, these lives, is the Church, embracing both.

To say this is an uncomfortable place to be is an understatement. Indeed, when I consider the scissor graphs describing the injustices in our educational landscape, and see the effects of these disparities in the lives of children— rich, poor and in the diminishing middle class—I see crosses where Jesus's arms of love for all God's children are extended ever wider.

CHAPTER TEN

They Were Reading on the Bus

R. William Franklin

To learn to read is to light a fire.

—Victor Hugo, *Les Miserables*

One of the most wonderful moments of my entire ministry as a bishop happened during the summer of 2015. I was in the basement meeting room of our Diocesan Ministry Center, sitting at a piano playing songs that many of us remember from childhood. Songs like "Twinkle, Twinkle Little Star" and "Go Tell Aunt Rhody." Children from the city of Buffalo and teenagers from Virginia and New Jersey surrounded me. They started off a little tentative, but by the end they were singing along. As I got up to leave, one of the girls asked me when I was going to bring her some coffee, and everyone laughed. The children were participants in the Eaton Summer Reading program, and the teenagers were spending a week on a mission trip helping with the program.

Like most of the best things, it didn't start with the idea for a summer reading program. It didn't even start with a thought about education. It started with a book. A group of clergy in Western New York had been reading the book *Toxic Charity* by Robert Lupton, and had gotten together to discuss it.

The conversation was wide ranging and moved from our congregations to generational poverty to equality of opportunity to racism to the specifics of those issues in the Buffalo Niagara region and back again. The only things that were clear were that the issues were complex and we, as a diocese, needed to do something. A small group agreed to get together and keep talking.

There is certainly plenty of need in the Buffalo Niagara region. The group actually started with the idea of helping to change our food pantries and pet food pantries into co-ops. They also talked a lot about the possibility of a credit union or similar project to address the issue of underbanking and payday lending. They talked about a one-stop shop for several different types of services because transportation, or the lack of it, is a serious issue here. They talked about job training and interview practice to help people get the jobs that economic redevelopment was starting to bring to our region. However, the conversation kept coming back to education.

The Buffalo Public Schools are notorious. They are dysfunctional and have been for more than a generation. As the group was talking, story after story was appearing in the press that underlined that the public schools and educational inequality was one major factor in the continuing of generational poverty and economic inequality in our region. The group began to do some research to put some facts with their impressions. The facts were worse than any of us thought.

In Buffalo, only 11.5 percent of students in third through eighth grade met or exceeded New York State proficiency standards in English. In math, only 9.6 percent met or exceeded standards. The general high school graduation rate in the Buffalo schools was less than 50 percent and for young men of color the graduation rate was less than 25 percent.

The group found many studies that showed that a student's reading level by the end of grade 3 is a direct indicator of whether or not they will graduate, which is to say that children reading below level when they are nine years old will not graduate when they are seventeen years old. This is true because the end of grade 3 is a time when children shift from learning to read to reading to learn. Study after study also shows that the ability to read and to understand what is read is the fundamental skill needed to escape from the cycle of generational poverty.

This seemed like the perfect place for our diocese to try to break the cycle of poverty.

While at first the problem seems overwhelming, one obvious place for intervention is in elementary school reading. The research is clear: summer enrichment programs positively impact the reading levels of children living in poverty. If young children's reading levels are able to be improved sustainably, it can break the cycle of poverty, because it will set them up for further success in school, high school graduation, and provide them with the ability to obtain better paying jobs. The better the education of the parent, the better the education of the child who will be able to live above the poverty line. In fact, intervening on the elementary level with a focus on reading can have a generational effect on healing intergenerational poverty in families.

We had some of the tools already. Like most dioceses, the Diocese of Western New York has congregations full of people who love to read. More than three quarters of the members of our congregations have postsecondary educations. We have congregations full of teachers, retired teachers, librarians, retired librarians, and many, many others who know the value of reading and who love to read. We also have a Ministry Center with plenty of space both indoors and out. We had a priest who also had a social work degree and a heart for children who was willing to serve as the director of the program. We had priests, deacons, and laypeople with education and literacy backgrounds who were willing to serve on a board for the program. We had congregations with relationships with public schools who could get information about the camp to the children.

We started making plans. We looked at the Reading Camp[3] that the Diocese of Lexington had pioneered. It seemed like a good model, but we thought one week was not enough, and we couldn't do an overnight program for the children since we didn't have a "camp." We hit on the idea of pairing our summer reading program with the mission trips that are a part of the youth program of so many congregations and dioceses. If we could have local adult volunteers to teach, and teenagers, both local and from other places, spend a week on a mission trip as junior counselors, we would have all the staffing we needed. The program would be a day camp for the children. The youth could live in the upstairs of our Ministry Center, and the program would happen downstairs.

---

3. See https://www.readingcamprocks.org.

We came up with the plan. We would run a five-week summer day camp focusing on reading and literacy skills with enrichment and field trips. It seemed like a huge challenge, but also something we could do if we tried hard enough. It also seemed like a way that we could make a difference in the lives of people in our region.

We started putting together concrete plans. We thought that we would open our program to fifty children from the Buffalo Public Schools who had just finished kindergarten, first, second, or third grade. We started putting together budgets and lists of things that we would need. We wanted the program to run from 8:00 a.m. to 5:00 p.m. each day so parents would not need additional day care. We thought that we might need to raise $50,000 for the first year. That seemed like a goal that we could reach.

In the midst of this, Jim Eaton, our longtime diocesan treasurer, died after a long battle with cancer. Jim was an amazing man; his life and his faith impacted many people. We were searching for a way to honor him.

Jim had been one of the driving forces behind the creation of our diocesan Ministry Center. He had a vision of the building as a place where the diocese could come together and do ministry. Jim also was passionate about Buffalo and about education. He had an elementary school in Buffalo that he had adopted. They even made him principal for a day. I can't believe how long it took us to put the pieces together and name our program the "Jim Eaton Summer Reading Program," Eaton Camp for short.

We continued to make plans. There were hurdles and things we hadn't considered. We needed more money than we had originally thought. And people got excited about it. We had a table at our 2014 and 2015 Diocesan Conventions asking people to donate books. We had nearly 250 books donated in twenty-four hours. We had congregations do fundraisers and toilet paper collections. (We knew we'd need a lot of toilet paper.) We had volunteers sign up and come to training. It was starting to happen.

Do you know the old saying, "Man makes plans and God laughs"? That is the story of the first year of Eaton Camp.

We had thought we would have fifty children enrolled. We were very disappointed before it began that there were only twelve when we started; it went up to eighteen over the course of the summer, but some left too. It turns out that God had a plan. We had underestimated how much attention each child would need. Our final enrollment numbers allowed us give each child one-on-one and sometimes more than one-on-one attention and that is exactly what was needed.

How do we explain these numbers? While the need for summer reading enrichment in Buffalo is high, the infrastructure to offer such enrichment is depleted. In our inaugural year 2015 we had the explicit promise of support (with registration, with books, with curriculum) from the "Say Yes Buffalo" program.[4] This promise was not fulfilled, leading us to "downsize" our program. What we learned is that the children's myriad educational, social, and physical needs required one-on-one attention, attention they would not have received had our enrollment been higher.

We learned how important a bus monitor is. We learned that structure and routine are crucial. We learned that children will do almost anything to get a prize. We learned that Mayor Brown's summer reading program is a fantastic motivator. The Buffalo Mayor's Summer Reading Challenge is in its fifteenth year; over 10,000 Buffalo Public School students have participated. For students in pre-K to third grade, the goal is to read seven books over the summer. Each participant must write a book report of at least ten sentences on each book that is read. All successful participants are invited to a huge celebration where awards and prizes are distributed.

Our first week was a little rough, but we learned and the children learned. We developed routines, and I learned not to promise the children anything. I was carrying my coffee mug when I came to visit and the children asked if they could have some coffee. I told them that I would bring them some sometime. After that every time I came over, they asked if I had brought them coffee. That's because I always had a coffee cup with me!

We learned other things too. We learned that, as valuable as the lessons that we had planned were, the free time was more valuable. For most of these children this was the only place in their lives where they had both safety and agency.

In their schools they are, most of the time, safe, but they are very limited in the choices they can make. They have no agency. In their homes they often have more agency, but they are often not safe. Their neighborhoods are not safe. What happens at home and school? The children, having

---

4. "Say Yes to Education" is a nationwide initiative to send more inner-city students to college. See http://sayyestoeducation.org.

been encouraged, valued, and honored during the Eaton Summer Reading Program, stood up for themselves at home, waking parents or guardians up each morning so they could get to school on time. In school they were more confident and engaged.

What this meant was that free time at camp, where they had a choice of ten different games to play, a library full of books to read, pillows that they could make forts out of, craft materials they could use, and many people who were willing to play with them, was as valuable a learning time as any of our workshop rotations.

We learned that having extra teenagers just hanging around reading books was an important thing. The children saw young people who they thought were cool and interesting reading by choice and that led to some of the children reading by choice.

We learned that stuffed animals are important and that children will read books to large tigers. We learned that children need to eat often and that naptime is a good thing, even for ten-year-olds.

We learned that interacting with children all day is hard work. We learned that we needed to give our director a half-day off during the week and that we needed to give our missioners time off during the day.

We learned that having a book each week, a book that we read over and over, was very important. We learned that it was very important that they got to take that book home. On the Friday of the next to last week of the program on their way home on the bus, the children got out the books they had been reading all week and started to read them. All on their own. The bus monitor held her breath, but they kept reading all the way home. The bus monitor sent us all an e-mail that evening with the subject line, "They were reading on the bus!" The picture of those children reading on the bus is one of my favorites. It is an icon of changed lives.

Success is hard to measure, but we have some data and some stories:

On each child's first day of camp we used the common core sight words for kindergarten and first grade and got a baseline of how many of the sight words they knew. On the last week of camp we went through the sight words again. No child had lost any sight words, and all but one child not only had gained sight words, but also knew all of the first grade sight words. Some of them had some of the second grade sight words. Learning gains over the summer is almost unheard of for children living in poverty, but that is what we saw. Every child in the Eaton program wrote seven book reports for the Mayor's summer reading program in Buffalo.

The best measure comes from a report from one of our most difficult children.

The Eaton program happened to come up in conversation with a school social worker. The social worker reported that this child, who had been reading below grade level at the end of second grade, came into third grade reading at grade level and, more importantly, his teacher reported that he was choosing to read in his free time. That young man now thinks of himself as a capable reader and chooses to read. We have changed this young man's life in measurable ways.

We are making plans for 2016, our second year. We are moving the children's part of the program to one of our churches in the city, walking distance from the zoo and Delaware Park. We are recruiting volunteers, youth missioners, and children. We are collecting toilet paper and paper plates. We are revising curriculum based on the Episcopal Diocese of Lexington's Reading Camp Program and raising money.

It is clear to me that breaking the cycle of poverty one child at a time is perhaps the most important thing that the Diocese of Western New York has ever done.

PART FIVE

Partnerships of Church and School

CHAPTER ELEVEN

Giving Up Outreach Projects

Hal Ley Hayek and Amy Slaughter Myers

Just then a lawyer stood up to test Jesus. "Teacher," he said, "what must I do to inherit eternal life?" He said to him, "What is written in the law? What do you read there?" He answered, "You shall love the Lord your God with all your heart, and with all your soul, and with all your strength, and with all your mind; and your neighbor as yourself." And he said to him, "You have given the right answer; do this, and you will live."

—Luke 10:25–37

C hurch-school partnerships aim at nothing less than living out the radical vision of the gospel. They compel the church to be engaged as a neighbor with the local public school community. The children and youth within a congregation are no different than the children and youth being formed in the public schools around our congregations. We are all children of God. The adults in our churches are no different in the eyes of God than those in the families of these same public school children. We may hear the gospel mandate to love our neighbor in worship; we may study the gospel mandate to love our neighbor in Bible study and adult formation offerings in church, but we *must act* as neighbors for the gospel to be alive in our neighborhoods and *in our congregations*. The gospel renews the congregation when it *acts as* a neighbor to its local public school. In such a relationship, the congregation confronts its own neediness, its own powerlessness, its own limits of love and care, and in so doing, becomes more deeply formed as Christian community, as followers of Jesus. Befriending public schools nourishes and revitalizes congregations, growing them in spirit and action.

Church-School Partnerships as Christian Formation

A paradigm of Christian formation can be imagined as the cross: each dimension of the cross represents an intentional practice that followers of Jesus must engage in to grow into the full stature of Christ.[1] The four dimensions of the cross point to four pairs of practices: prayer/listening, study/research, mission/action, and liturgy/evaluation. Seeing intentional spiritual practices (the first in each pair) through the lens of community organizing practices (the second in each pair) creates a synergy that awakens the soul and gives a witness to the world. These pairings create a formation experience that gives flesh to the dynamic of contemplative and active behavior.

We came to this insight from years of collaborative work and study both within congregations and in neighborhoods. What initially seemed disconnected areas—formation inside the church and outreach outside the church—are in fact mutually reinforcing in often surprising ways. This insight and resulting change of practice drew us deeper into our faith journey

Just as the cross is incomplete if one piece is missing, Christian formation is incomplete if any one pair of these practices is neglected in favor of the others. Prayer grounds us in our relationship with God and with each other, reminding us to listen to God and to each other. Study links us to the people of God who have gone before whose witness is found in Scripture and tradition. Study also leads us to research the congregation's local context, stirring us to reflect on how the Holy Spirit is at work in that local context. Action in the world with our neighbors for the common good draws us deeper into our baptismal promise to strive for justice and peace, joining in the mission of the wider church. Liturgy is a time for thanksgiving and communal evaluation of our lives and our journey to wholeness as Christian people and Christian community. Using the cross as an image of Christian formation foregrounds the fact that all these practices are necessary for growth. The image of the

---

1. Ephesians 4:13.

cross prevents us from becoming too rigidly focused on one point—liturgy, say, or Bible study—and thus blinded to the full vision of Christian discipleship, what Jesus invites us into when he tells us "follow me." As an image of Christian formation, the cross is made alive not as a symbol of execution but as the vibrant Tree of Life for all.

Prayer/Listening

In 1997, Baltimore was grieved by the death of three-year-old James Smith III, killed by a stray bullet in a barber shop as he sat in his mother's lap for his birthday haircut. This senseless death is only one of many such senseless deaths in Baltimore, and yet it is this death that started the congregation of the Episcopal Cathedral of the Incarnation on its path to partnership with public schools.

Listening as a practice is a spiritual exercise that gives life to human community. It is a mutual action that opens the listener up to the other person—their hopes, passions, material needs, and life context. Humility and mutual listening must guide church-school partnerships. What does the public school need or want? The Episcopal Cathedral of the Incarnation began its partnership with public schools at the material level. In Baltimore, over 80 percent of students qualify for free or reduced-priced lunch. School supplies drives, uniform drives, socks and underwear, mitten trees—all provide much needed resources to schools serving families in need, and for many years the Cathedral engaged in such drives almost without a second thought. It became a habit, a response to what the congregation had heard many years ago from its partner public schools.

Then, in 2013, Cathy Miles, principal of Abbottston Elementary School, challenged the congregation to listen more deeply to school staff and families. She told leaders in the congregation that she had local businesses and community groups donating supplies; it was fairly easy for her to get such donations. What the school didn't have were enough caring adults in the classroom. Parent-teacher conferences were often not well attended because of parents' work commitments or the stress that characterized many of the students' families. She asked for adults to be present at these conferences, to listen to the students with the teachers as they shared their schoolwork and their hopes for the school year. Like Jesus, this principal invited the congregation to a deeper relationship with God and neighbor through listening.

This principal challenged the congregation to deepen relationships with students, families, and staff. Did we as a congregation have the capacity to go deeper? The congregation had to be honest with itself and embarked on a listening campaign to discover the hopes, passions, and dreams of the congregation as it sought to follow Jesus. As a member congregation of Baltimoreans United in Leadership Development (BUILD),[2] Cathedral leadership engaged BUILD to design and run a listening campaign—a time-limited, focused effort of listening to each other in one-on-one meetings—within the congregation. This listening campaign strengthened our relationships and provided a way for newcomers to be integrated. The invitation of one public school principal to listen to her school's needs developed our capacity to listen more deeply to one another, thus forming us more deeply as Christians.

We know we are listening when we hear our own story in other people's story of their life and struggles. We know we are listening when our study tells us what must change for equity, justice, and right to rule in our neighborhood. We do not get stuck in our church, but, like the travellers on the Jericho Road in Luke's parable of the Good Samaritan,[3] we enter into risky and vulnerable places, opening us up to spiritual growth.

Study/Research

The congregation comes to reflect on how it might develop and nurture a congregation of mission-aware people and engage its neighborhood public school through Bible study of how Jesus engages with those around him. Lectionary and thematic Bible studies are important, but congregations must also intentionally encounter the biblical text through the lens of their local context. The Bible tells us that *all* children are part of God's community of the beloved. Study and research forms us most deeply as Christians when we connect the civic issues of our local context, particularly those of public schools and issues of equity and justice, with the reconciling work of the Holy Spirit.

One outcome of our listening campaign was the 2013 Advent Bible study. The Outreach team and the Christian Formation team sat down together and looked at the biblical texts for the season. The teams found a common theme: light coming into the world that changes the world. From this study

---

2. Baltimore's Industrial Areas Foundation affiliate, www.buildiaf.org.
3. Luke 10:25–37.

they organized a multigenerational formation forum featuring people from Baltimore whose stories told of being that light and making change in neighborhoods for the better. The Outreach and Christian Formation teams then challenged the congregation to consider where it might engage more deeply in Baltimore.

Each moment in the life of the church-school relationship is Christian formation for the whole congregation. School supplies and uniform drives are Christian formation when they are accompanied by opportunities for corporate reflection on these drives: Why are so many families in our local public school living at or below the federal poverty level? What might we as a congregation learn about our own neighborhood when we research such a question? How might we incorporate what we learn in worship and liturgy?

If the school asks for class volunteers from the congregation, those volunteers can gather and reflect on those experiences together as a form of study and prayer. How might that be shared? Such questions and the study needed to answer them is hard work for congregations. Exploring such questions honestly may open up real disagreements in the congregation about how Christians are to act ethically in the public sphere. These disagreements, when guided by humility and mutual listening, can open up the congregation to vital reflection on what it means to be followers of Jesus in this time and place.

In the parable of the Good Samaritan, Jesus tells us that if we love God we must *encounter* our neighbors and *practice* our neighborliness as a community of the faithful. Each congregation must confront how it should practice its neighborliness. Partnerships with public schools provide opportunities for learning how to act as neighbor, how to care for those around us respecting our diverse religious and cultural identities without being separated by them, how to risk being vulnerable in places we do not control, how to grow closer to God through listening to what our neighbor needs and wants. It is in this deepest sense that the church-school relationship is a tool for Christian formation and the spiritual life. The congregation has the opportunity to *act* as neighbors and then *reflect* on that action corporately: What's working in the church-school partnership? What's failing? What needs nurture and what needs to be let go? How do we discern that in community? How do we work through the inevitable conflicts, disagreements, and difficulties relating to others who are not of our religion or culture or education or income level? How do we confront our own biases? How do we know we are *really* listening to God and neighbor in this work? These tensions embraced honestly are life-giving and a source of renewal for congregations.

Mission/Action

For the Cathedral of the Incarnation, it took many years of clothing and school supplies drives, of tutors and classroom volunteers sharing their experiences to prompt a congregation-wide conversation about why such drives and volunteers seemed to be necessary. By then, the Cathedral had been partnering with two local public schools for more than eight years. Waverly Elementary / Middle School had been promised a new school building by the Baltimore City School Board in 2003, but breaking ground had been postponed year after year. Why was it so difficult to get a much-needed new school facility built in the city when the process went so much more smoothly in surrounding counties?

Research and reflection on these questions confronted the congregation with uncomfortable realities of class and race: whatever our individual views were, we had to come to a shared commitment as a congregation to stand effectively with our public school partners. By 2007, members of the congregation had met with elected and appointed officials, written letters and e-mails, and attended key community meetings to ensure that this promised school building was fully funded and a construction date set. Occupation of the new school by students was anticipated in December of 2013. In this way, the congregation experienced firsthand the need for wider partnerships to meet the call of equity and justice in public schools.

Annual cuts to the city's school budget prompted the Cathedral in 2009 to join with neighborhood associations, schools, and other nonprofits, in the Baltimore Education Coalition to prevent such cuts. This experience in turn prodded many in the congregation to ask about the state of school facilities across Baltimore. Why must Baltimore fight in order to get the kind of school buildings all children deserve and that are frequently found less than a mile away in Baltimore County without such a fight? In 2011, the Cathedral became a founding member of Transform Baltimore, the campaign to make renovating and modernizing all public school buildings in Baltimore within eight years the top priority of elected and appointed officials at the city and state level.

Action in the world draws congregations into relationship with those with whom they might not always wish to be in relationship: secular institutions, neighborhood associations, politicians across the spectrum, corporate and foundation leaders, elected and appointed officials. Practicing neighborliness with these organizations and groups deepened opportunities for reflection and formation. Congregations are thereby drawn into the tension of either being neighbors or passing by, like the priest and the Levite in the parable of the Good Samaritan. The priest and the Levite had good reasons not to attend to the dying man on the Jericho Road, but Jesus clearly teaches that we should imitate the intervention of the Samaritan to have eternal life. Congregations must be actively engaged in honest dialogue about the welfare of the wider community. Congregations must have relationships with local elected and appointed officials to hold them accountable to the vision for the community.

Liturgy/Evaluation

In response to the 1997 tragic death of James Smith III, the Cathedral of the Incarnation began to remember each Baltimore child killed by violence by name in its weekly worship service. The remembrance was practiced by lighting a candle at the altar and then during the recessional a child of the congregation would carry the candle to the Children's Altar. This regular liturgical practice created an environment of accountability—of self-evaluation—through communal action and kept our mission before us. This process of evaluation formed the congregation that gathered at the Cathedral, a congregation of people from Baltimore and surrounding counties, as well as from across the rest of Maryland who attended the Cathedral for special diocesan services. For many years, these remembrance candles were retired on January 1st, the Feast of the Holy Innocents, marking the story of when King Herod ordered all male infants be killed in a failed attempt to kill "the child who has been born king of the Jews."[4] The Collect appointed for this feast day reminds the worshipping community of God's interest in justice on earth: "Receive, we pray, into the arms of your mercy all innocent victims; and by your great might frustrate the designs of evil tyrants and establish your rule of justice, love, and peace."[5] The liturgy challenges us to step outside ourselves and join with others committed to the same work.

Starting in January 2010, we engaged the interfaith community of Baltimore as an act of mutual accountability to address the violence in our

---

4. Matthew 2:2.
5. Book of Common Prayer, 238.

neighborhoods. Every year we renewed our common commitment by pledging to end violence as we read the names and remembered each child killed the previous year. In these worship services, the ever-present reality of violence in the lives of Baltimore's children was made present and real to those of us who were shielded from such violence in our daily lives. Remembering and praying for these young victims of violence grounded the liturgy in Baltimore's reality: in 2015 there were 344 homicides, the second highest number recorded. Twenty-five of those who died by violence were children under the age of eighteen.

As congregations, we must pray for and remember both the victims and the perpetrators of violence in our communities. Each congregation is called to be a congregation in a particular place and time; the Prayers of the People reflect the needs and concerns of the congregation that is gathered there and then. But to be a congregation today in Freddie Gray's Baltimore demands that the congregation does more than pray and remember. The congregation must move from *praying for* its neighbors to *acting with* its neighbors to confront violence and injustice. The congregation is called from its worship into the city, to enter into the pain and suffering at the heart of so much of its violence, and to act as neighbors to public schools.

Public schools are those institutions that are required by law to serve all children in the neighborhood. Congregations are called to be in relationship with their public schools, not as a service project or outreach program, not as a separate activity a few people in church do outside of worship or on their own, not as an add-on or option in the practice of Christian discipleship, but rather as fundamental work of being followers of Jesus in community. Our liturgy serves as an evaluation as we confess our deeds done and deeds left undone as Christian community. Such partnerships look like a relationship between equals, between institutions charged with care and formation of human beings, between friends. Jesus said, "You are my friends if you do what I command you."[6]

---

6. John 15:14.

CHAPTER TWELVE

Transforming Mission

Alexizendria Link

When schools, families, and community groups work together to support learning, children tend to do better in school, stay in school longer, and like school more.

—"A New Wave of Evidence," Southwest
Educational Development Laboratory

I'm a proud member of St. Luke's Episcopal Church in Worcester, Massachusetts. We are described by the parish as a church that comes "from many backgrounds and perspectives, but we share two common commitments: to grow in our faith and to grow in our love of God and our neighbors." A small Episcopal neighborhood parish of around 150 to 175 parishioners, our faith is abundant in comparison to the numbers of worshippers each Sunday. Our different backgrounds and perspectives often shape how we seek and serve God, yet each Sunday we drink from the same cup, praise the same God, and live with the same hope of growing in our faith. Christian formation is important to members of St. Luke's. We "seek to serve the world in Jesus' name as we worship, learn, grow and journey along the disciple's way with Jesus Christ."

Although I have an extensive history with the Episcopal Church, I've only been attending St. Luke's for three years, because I've only lived in the city for a short time. I came to Worcester to teach in an urban charter school. I struggled at first making my way in the city. Worcester is the second largest city in Massachusetts with demographics similar to Boston's. We have nationally recognized colleges and universities, diverse cultures, and multibillion dollar public and private investments. There is also an obvious racial and class divide throughout the city. Worcester has a large immigrant and refugee population and has become a settlement city for different cultures that have come to the United States.

Having a community organizing background, I assumed the social service agencies, schools, churches, and nonprofit organizations would be the way for me to adjust in Worcester. Although I wasn't surprised, I was challenged by the disparities in education and employment across culture and class throughout the city. I found several social services weren't as culturally competent as I thought necessary to address issues that affected the social and emotional learning and the mental health concerns of students in communities of color.

In addition to transitioning to a new city, I also arrived at St. Luke's during a time the congregation was in transition. I had visited multiple Episcopal churches for over a year (including St. Luke's) before I decided it was the perfect match for me. During my church exploration, St. Luke's rector resigned, was followed by an interim, and our current priest-in-charge was assigned. It was interesting to watch the dynamics of parishioners, myself included, as we searched for our new leader. Although there were differences of opinion, similar to our church demographics, our faith was stronger than ever.

The Reverend Timothy H. Burger came to us with a ministry that includes the integration of arts and spirituality, a charismatic personality, devoted preaching, refreshing energy, and an intentional commitment to Christian formation. Soon after he arrived, our bishop, the Right Reverend Douglas Fisher, appointed a new deacon to St. Luke's, the Reverend Donna Kingman. There is new energy at our small parish that has been so fulfilling to many of us. The words "Jesus Movement" are frequently heard from the pulpit and throughout the church, and we have begun having forums and discussions between services about our faith and ministry.

A Partnership with All Our Children

It didn't take long for members at St. Luke's and other parishes in Worcester to begin collaborating to participate in All Our Children. In fact, the desire and subsequent action to form a chapter came up organically one Sunday during coffee hour. Deacon Kingman mentioned her disappointment at not being able to attend "Following Jesus into Your Neighborhood: Serving All God's Children," a February 2016 conference presented in collaboration with Province I and All Our Children. She spoke of her regret with no idea I had attended the conference. Ironically, I still had materials in my purse. Imagine our delight and surprise when I was able to produce documents on the spot! We immediately began talking about the possibilities, while other church members listened in. Both Donna and I have backgrounds in theology and education; more importantly we are both grounded in the role our faith plays in our occupation, daily lives, and passion for good.

We naturally began to think of ways to coordinate community resources while also valuing the power of how cultural, civic, and religious organizations could partner to improve school outcomes and provide support. After teaching for four years in the charter school, I transferred into the public school system, which brought me heightened awareness of how institutional and systematic structures and policies differently affected students. I identify the disparities in education, which is exacerbating levels of inequality and negatively impacting the lives of children, as a social justice issue. To paraphrase Frederick Buechner: our own ministry is discovered at the intersection—at the place of meeting—between our own greatest passion and the world's greatest need. I suppose it is the vocation of every individual to imagine and discern where this place is for them.

Most individuals realize there is economic inequality in society and the disparity continues to grow. Throughout the United States, schools are economically segregated; the state of urban schooling is often directly related to dynamics of race, class, and culture. There is no dispute regarding the lack of adequate education in economically challenged areas and communities of color. As a classroom educator, I experienced and witnessed the same systematic and institutional forms of racism found in society were also prominent in schools. Some teachers subconsciously lowered educational standards for youth of color, lacked the patience and understanding of their culture, and imposed more punitive forms of discipline on them. These were not deliberate acts of discrimination or injustice, but residual effects of bias and lack of awareness or exposure to cultural norms other than their own.

The early stages of the All Our Children partnership in Worcester has been rewarding. St. Luke's knows that education provides more opportunity for every citizen and can provide upward mobility and understanding. When the church disengages in identifying education as social justice, the church abdicates its voice to call for society to provide adequate education for its most vulnerable and disadvantaged communities. Social justice is defined as "promoting a just society by challenging injustice and valuing diversity." It exists when "all people share a common humanity and therefore have a right to equitable treatment, support for their human rights, and a fair allocation of community resources."[7] St. Luke's has embraced the desire to live into the concept of a common humanity.

Our Baptism and God's Mission

The most significant role that Christians can play to address the root problem of educational disparities is to be present, knowing we don't have the answers yet being willing to listen and provide support. This ministry of presence means we are servants who support, not leaders who need to control. Instead, we know our religious communities and organizations can offer valuable resources and opportunities to create access for building alliances, creating partnerships, developing leadership, and confronting and challenging oppressive practices that are deeply embedded in our society. By tapping into our spiritual gifts and talents as a parish, St Luke's became a vehicle of access for students in the city. Our rector's love and sense of the arts generated a rebirth of gifts and talents of our parishioners. We have retired educators, singers, painters, handymen, accountants, businessmen and women, nonprofit professionals, community board members, computer experts, homemakers, gardeners, and many more. All of whose talents, when shared, become a source of access and experience for others and share in the humanity of all.

---

7. Cyndy Caravelis and Matthew Robinson, *Social Justice, Criminal Justice: The Role of American Law in Effecting and Preventing Social Change* (New York: Routledge, 2016), 8.

Through my studies at the Episcopal Divinity School, I learned mission is summed up in the *Missio Dei*.[8] God has a mission, and that mission is to seek us. God's seeking has two aims: our salvation—that is, freeing us from sins and restoring us to a right relationship with God—and our liberation—breaking the power of sin in earthly structures and relationships and restoring right relationships among people. Mission may also mean the events and programs, the ways and means the church expresses God's call, or its sense of its purpose for existing. God's mission for us will vary in size, number, and timeframes. St. Luke's participates as a church in God's mission through our support of All Our Children.

The All Our Children initiative has allowed me to reflect on what God's mission has meant to—and is—for me. My experiences, heritage, and culture are all incorporated in my uniqueness and spirituality and how I carry out mission. This is true for everyone, and our individual experiences enhance the lives of one another. Additionally, our baptismal covenant invites us to be a Christian witness and share the gifts we have. An important underlying principle of the ministry of the baptized is that "every Christian community is blessed with the gifts it requires for effective ministry and mission."[9] While it is human nature for parishes to discount our ability to affect communities and cultures outside our comfort zone, doing so relinquishes our own power.

In reality we are enough. We are more than enough when we listen and respond without preconceived notions and expectations from others. Congregations and volunteers can discern God's call collectively or individually and reflect on how God is leading us in our baptismal calling.

Partnerships Are Needed

Although St. Luke's is in the early stages of our partnerships, we are excited about the possibilities and interest throughout the community and diocese. Our partnerships are developing with Episcopal churches, a nonprofit for

---

8. My thinking here is influenced by David J. Bosch in *Transforming Mission: Paradigm Shifts in Theology of Mission* (Maryknoll, NY: Orbis, 1991).

9. Sheryl A. Kujawa-Holbrook and Fredrica Harris Thompsett, *Born of the Water, Born of the Spirit: Supporting Ministry of the Baptized in a Small Congregation* (Herndon, VA: Alban Institute, 2010), 64.

education, and an urban public school in a challenging area of Worcester, each of which has different needs. Partnerships with the African Community Education (ACE) and Claremont Academy will allow parishioners to participate at their own comfort and commitment level under the umbrella of All Our Children.

The mission of ACE is to assist African refugee and immigrant youth and families in achieving educational and social stability through access to academic support, leadership development, cultural expression, and community. ACE aims to achieve this mission by providing academic and non-academic programming during after-school and out-of-school time. They currently use experienced teachers and enthusiastic volunteers to support students' needs as they move toward high school graduation and postsecondary success. Parishioners at St. Luke's are forming and signing on to be part of the volunteer effort.

Claremont Academy is a public high school in Worcester. Most of the students self-identify as Asian, Hispanic, or multiracial, and 90 percent of all students qualify for free or reduced lunch. Some of the students from Claremont also benefit from ACE programming. Recently there has been an influx of refugee students at the school, and St. Luke's is passionate in supporting them.

Once we begin working fully with our partnered school and community organization, we plan to provide heightened awareness and understanding to our congregation and throughout the Diocese of Western Massachusetts. There is so much joy in participating in partnerships that honor communities, culture, and diversity. Not only does working with All Our Children assist our ability to coexist in society and participate in a shared humanity, it provides ongoing spiritual formation and mission while experiencing God's grace throughout.

Unlike government and federal agencies, religious and most nonprofit organizations are not bound to the political climate and practices that contribute to complex political constructs in urban and rural environments. Often schools that reside in these areas are faced with political paradigms that fail to address larger contexts such as social, economic, mental health, and political issues. Additionally, societal issues outside of the educational environment affect schooling through the unequal distribution of educational opportunities.

On February 5, 2009, President Barack Obama signed an executive order establishing the new White House Office of Faith-Based and Neighborhood Partnerships. This Office is dedicated to working on behalf of Americans committed to improving their communities, no matter their religious or political beliefs. President Obama said:

> The change that Americans are looking for will not come from government alone. There is a force for good greater than government. It is an expression of faith, this yearning to give back, this hungering for a purpose larger than our own, that reveals itself not simply in places of worship, but in senior centers and shelters, schools and hospitals, and any place an American decides.[10]

The state of education today is requiring a response that moves beyond the traditional way of supporting schools. In *Beyond the Bake Sale: The Essential Guide to Family/School Partnerships*, Karen Mapp places emphasis on engaging all community members with an interest in education to be part of collaborative efforts to improve the system. Democratic accountability in schools should bring about equity and inclusion for all children; however this doesn't always happen. All Our Children is a resource grounded in spiritual formation, education, and training that promotes ways to assist with equity supports. Focusing more on the teachers' needs could greatly affect their ability to be more effective as well.

A Sanctuary for Teachers

St. Luke's hopes to be a sanctuary and support for teachers as well students. Our goal is to assist educators like me by alleviating some of the difficult dimensions of teaching. We at St. Luke's realize teacher efficacy is directly linked to teachers' psychological state in and outside the classroom. Faith values aligned with physical support is a ministry of presence; the Church can be that ministry for teachers who are often overworked and underpaid. As someone with a theological and education background, I'm aware we need to continue to think of ways to improve the conditions of everyone in

---

10. "Obama Announces White House Office of Faith-based and Neighborhood Partnerships," *The White House*, February 5, 2009, https://www.whitehouse.gov/the-press-office/obama -announces-white-house-office-faith-based-and-neighborhood-partnerships.

society. In other words, "knowledge emerges only through invention and re-invention, through the restless, impatient, continuing, hopeful inquiry human beings pursue in the world, with the world, and with each other."[11] All Our Children is the hopeful and faithful inquiry to see the face of God in others and participate in God's reconciling mission to the world in Jesus Christ.

Working as a parish to begin and build an All Our Children partnership is among our current Christian formation goals at St. Luke's. We consider Christian formation a lifelong process of growing our relationship with God, self, others, and all creation. Every experience in our lives can provide us with the opportunity to express our faith. The challenge we face is to recognize these opportunities when they arise and learning ways to live with heightened cultural awareness in a secular world. All Our Children is contributing to our ability to participate with cognizance in relationships that we may not otherwise experience.

---

11. Paulo Freire, *Pedagogy of the Oppressed* (New York: Herder & Herder, 1971), 72.

CHAPTER THIRTEEN

The Journey

Ruth Wong

The Christian faith is based upon being committed to God's dream for us personally and communally. Our living creatively into the future involves our devotion to the compelling vision of God's realm of shalom.
—Luther E. Smith, *Living into God's Dream*

How does a Chinese-American immigrant, who spent twelve years of her life in Taiwan and grew up mostly in nondenominational churches, become a mobilizer to help churches of all denominations and ethnicities collaborate with each other and build partnerships with schools? Especially in the context of doing this work in Boston, a city where I did not grow up, it seems all the more strange that someone like me would be considered to take on this role. Only through God's divine calling, preparation, and intervention could something like this happen. Just as Isaiah 55:8–9 (ESV) says:

> For my thoughts are not your thoughts,
> neither are your ways my ways, declares the Lord.
> For as the heavens are higher than the earth,
> so are my ways higher than your ways
> and my thoughts than your thoughts.

I attribute the small contributions I have been able to make completely to God. God's marvelous fingerprints are all over the journey and process that have shaped me to become a bridge builder and peacemaker through my role as the director of the Boston Education Collaborative (BEC) at Emmanuel Gospel Center. I look back and see that I have been prepared for this role and have been imparted a passion to see the Body of Christ reflect the "great multitude that no one could number, from every nation, from all tribes and peoples and languages, standing before the throne and before the Lamb,"[12] coming together to serve one another and with each other. The lenses through which I look at education and see the unique opportunity that churches have to love and serve their neighbors are shaped by my childhood experiences, through teaching in public schools, and from working with a range of church communities.

I spent my formative childhood and youth both in Taiwan and the northern suburbs of Chicago. Growing up as the daughter of parents who were lay leaders and teachers in their churches as well as other Christian ministries, I had the foundations of my faith, a biblical understanding of Scripture, and the example of Christian leadership laid firmly by my parents. I was able to observe how they led, taught, and discipled younger, emerging leaders. Their wisdom and discernment about church and ministry issues were inadvertently passed down to me. Having lived in multiple places and followed my parents around on many speaking trips, I was able to observe and experience a variety of churches.

While these experiences were limited to the Chinese church circles, other opportunities broadened my horizon to build relationships with people from backgrounds different than mine. I had opportunities to build friendships with classmates both abroad and from different cultures and ethnicities within the United States. I befriended the honor students as well as the theater students (not mutually exclusive, but they were mostly two different social circles). During my four years at Wellesley College (an institution that valued diversity), I attended and engaged in leadership opportunities at an urban Chinese church. However, on campus, I also intentionally chose to be involved in the InterVarsity Christian campus ministry and a Christian a cappella group,

---

12. Revelation 7:9 (ESV).

which expanded my Christian circle to friends of different racial, ethnic, and denominational backgrounds. I enjoyed fellowshipping with my Christian sisters and seeking that unity on campus as part of the same Body of Christ.

Two years later, when I made the decision to leave one racially and socio-economically homogeneous school district for a teaching job in another more heterogeneous district, I realized that my experiences from high school, college, and graduate school directly impacted my preference for and comfort in more diverse rather than less diverse settings.

It was also through my a cappella group that my vision for a more unified Christian body and voice began to grow. Those of us in the group attended different churches, came from different faith traditions, and represented to a certain degree, racial and cultural diversity. We all desired that the secular Wellesley community see Christians on campus represented not just by separate ministries and fellowships but also by one body that praised God together through our love for music.

After college, God used many years to develop and equip me as I worked with young people. During the eight years I taught high school, I learned to work with students of all backgrounds and learning styles, trying to vary ways of explaining challenging physics concepts or problem-solving techniques. While teaching I served for eight years as a college ministry counselor at two churches where I learned to facilitate sessions, lead Bible studies, mentor younger women, work with student leadership teams, and collaborate with counselors both within my church and from other churches. God used those years to prune me in my inner self as well as develop my interpersonal and leadership skills.

I believe that one of the key skills God refined in me (and continues to do so) were my listening skills. I had to listen well to students in both settings, whether to figure out how a physics concept was confusing to them or to hear students share their personal struggles in life. God also used those years to keep me humble. Teaching high school and serving in student ministries had their own unique set of student challenges each year. Many times, there were situations where I felt overwhelmed, lacking in wisdom, mistake-prone, and having no control over circumstances. The lessons in humility were much needed and precious to me. Christ's example of humility and not counting equality with God something to be grasped was and should be our model and aspiration in all that we do. Scripture says our selflessness and humility completes joy in others and ascribes glory to God.[13]

With all these experiences and lessons behind me, God brought me in the fall of 2006 to Emmanuel Gospel Center (EGC) for another stage of learning and equipping. As a seventy-plus-year-old Christian urban ministry, EGC had established long-standing trust with the greater Boston church communities across geographical, racial, denominational, and socioeconomic lines. I was plopped into a ministry with colleagues who had years of established relationships with Christian urban and suburban leaders, connections with many Christian networks, and years of ministry experience. EGC staff reflected the diversity of the wider Christian church in Boston, since it included different denominations, ethnicities, and generations. The opportunity to work with the diversity of the evangelical churches was made much simpler because I tapped into my colleagues as resources and built on the foundations that they had established. Being new to urban ministry, I took the first several years to be a sponge and immersed myself in learning and understanding urban systems.

An organization that desired to help churches and Christian leaders apply Living System Ministry principles, EGC provided me with fertile ground to deepen my understanding of social systems, especially the church and Boston education systems, while also seeking to find where the leverage points were for the church to make a difference in addressing educational inequities in our region.

Combined with a deepened systems understanding of the education landscape, a growing list of Christian faith-based programs and Christian youth workers, and a personal appreciation for how "the village" benefitted many of my former students who needed extra support, I became more and more convicted and passionate about connecting leaders to leaders, churches to churches, and churches to nonprofits, for the purpose of tapping into the wealth of experience and knowledge within the Christian community. I also saw the importance of connecting opportunities and resources from the secular nonprofit sector to help our churches and faith-based leaders strengthen the education or youth development work that they felt called to do. There

---

13. Philippians 2:1–9.

are over 2,000 nonprofits in the youth and education sector in Greater Boston,[14] so churches and programs do not need to recreate the wheel; they can access the knowledge and resources that these nonprofits provide. Many times, churches and leaders simply did not know about these resources. Furthermore, the Boston Education Collaborative (BEC) was learning from various models of how churches and Christians were engaging in education and youth development work. The BEC seeks to engage, network, and support Christian leaders and churches that care about urban education and youth development issues. BEC works with churches, schools, and nonprofits to empower underserved urban students with the education they need for transformation in their lives and in their communities. Many churches and leaders can often be siloed within their own programs or denominations. Why shouldn't churches learn from one another about best practices and models? It only seemed natural that churches and leaders should reach out to connect and even assist each other when they share the same visions for how to build up young people.

The Opportunity

The increased opportunity for churches to address educational needs in Boston through supporting public schools came about in 2010 when Dr. Carol Johnson, then Boston Public Schools superintendent, and Mayor Thomas Menino jointly announced the Circle of Promise initiative:

> The Circle of Promise, [was] a five mile geographic area in the heart of the City of Boston which [focused] on improving the economic and educational well-being of the families of children enrolled in the city's most challenged schools. This [was] an innovative, focused, and intentional strategy to work with parents who are finding it difficult to make ends meet by addressing individual family needs and facilitating access to Boston's wealth of community based agencies, faith based institutions, colleges and universities, and strong public and private sector organizations. The goal [was] to provide families with the support and

---

14. "Greater Boston's Nonprofit Sector," Massachusetts Nonprofit Network, March 2016, http://www.massnonprofitnet.org/wp-content/uploads/2016/03/Greater-Boston.pdf.

services needed to gain financial security in order for children to attain high academic achievement unabated.[15]

At the time, Dr. Johnson hired Dr. Brian Barnes, an ordained minister, former Boston Public Schools (BPS) teacher and administrator, to launch the community-based and faith-based initiative, inviting faith institutions to come alongside schools in the Circle of Promise area. Under Barnes's leadership, those of us who represented key faith-based networks (Jewish Community Relations Council, Greater Boston Interfaith Organization, the Black Ministerial Alliance, and Emmanuel Gospel Center) were invited to be part of an interfaith steering committee to envision what it would take to engage the larger faith community in Boston. I was able to support his work as a member of a subcommittee that researched national community-based and faith-based partnership models and created the materials that would be used to promote and execute the Circle of Promise initiative.

While some local churches and other faith institutions had been involved in supporting schools through direct service and advocacy work for many years, the intentionality and level of top-down support given by the BPS administration encouraged our area churches to join in the work of support-ing Boston schools. The position of a community liaison extended from 2010 through 2014, and supported the Office of Community Engagement and Circle of Promise to grow the number of faith-based partnerships.

For two years, I was contracted by BPS to serve as a community liai-son. One of my colleagues compared the work to that of a translator. With schools, I would "translate" the potential ways in which churches could come alongside as helpful partners. With churches, I would "translate" the needs and priorities of the schools using terms they could understand and explain how to navigate the complex school system. Prior to 2010, there may have been a handful of faith institutions that had partnerships with particular schools (no one was tracking at the time). By the end of 2014, about 20 per-cent of Boston's 128 schools had at least one faith-based partner. According to the BEC's tracking, by July 2016 at least 35 schools had one or more church

---

15. Mayor's Office, "Mayor Menino Launches Circle of Promise and LIFT-Boston Partnership to Move Families Forward." City of Boston. June 23, 2011, http://www.cityofboston.gov/news /default.aspx?id=5169.

partner(s) out of 125 schools, and there were at least 33 churches or church-affiliated programs involved in school partnerships.

With the support of a community liaison, the existence of an office of community engagement, and invitations to the semiannual partnership gatherings, there has been a sustained momentum of more churches wanting to get involved in partnering with the BPS. Furthermore, when Boston's new mayor, Marty Walsh, held his first clergy breakfast, some of the pastors spoke up and asked for his support of faith-based partnerships with schools. The Black Ministerial Alliance and EGC were able to ask for the new superintendent's support as we shared about the engagement of our churches and the numbers of churches and schools that were involved. Many BPS central office administrators were aware of the faith communities' involvement with schools and were supportive. With the level of visibility and support from the top, our churches in greater Boston should continue to have tremendous opportunities to serve Boston schools for many years to come. With existing examples and models of how churches can support Boston schools, more churches in cities and towns surrounding Boston have also joined in the movement.

The Body of Christ

BEC has been following the work of churches in their school partnerships and connecting nationally with other cities that have church-school partnership movements. We have found that the church-school partnerships in Boston have some different characteristics from the other cities across the United States. Unlike some cities that coordinate many more citywide events (like service days or donation drives), most of Boston's church-school partnerships have been individually tailored to serve the needs of one school, and we have only recently piloted a citywide service day as an outward expression of unity between our churches. Thus, all the Boston partnerships look different, which makes it challenging to find the impact our churches are making collectively.

While I assume collaboration between churches exists in other cities, I have not heard that narrative shared as clearly yet in our national conversations. However, in Boston it has been encouraging to see that almost one-third of the schools with a church partner have more than one church working with them. In many of these schools, churches are partnering with each other to serve the same school. Many of our church collaborations cross one or more of the geographic, racial, socioeconomic, or denominational lines. Some of them had previous relationships with each other that helped set the foundation for the collaboration. Others formed organically over time or through the BEC's efforts to connect them. In other cases, such as with St. Stephen's Episcopal Church,[16] the church coordinated opportunities to serve their school partner in a variety of ways so that other churches and organizations like EGC could participate.

At the Timilty Middle School, Peoples Baptist Church (a historically black church in Boston), North River Community Church (a mostly white suburban church south of Boston), and Congregación León de Judá (a mostly Latino church in Boston) form the Partnership for Excellence to come alongside and provide support. The churches have engaged in mentoring students, helping host and coordinate family events for the school, donating supplies, doing service projects, and bringing speakers from their congregations for career days. All three churches are equal partners with the school principal, and they meet monthly to share updates and plan ways to support the school.

Pastor Paul Atwater, senior pastor of North River Community Church, shared these thoughts about this partnership and why it is important for churches to be involved (his thoughts focus on Peoples Baptist and North River because the partnership began with these two churches; Congregación León de Judá fully joined the team several years later). He writes:

1. Serving in the Boston Public Schools allows us to become known for what we are for. How often we have heard that evangelical churches are too frequently known for what they are against. Serving in this way has allowed us to throw our weight into something that we all believe: that we are following the example of Jesus when we serve children. And this effort gives us common ground with the desires of the communities around us.

2. Serving in partnership enables us to more fully experience the richness of Christ's body. . . . Serving together has enriched the faith and experiences of both churches. The friendships today go far beyond that experienced by the two founding pastors.

---

16. See chapter 4 for more about St. Stephen's Episcopal Church.

3. Serving as partners for the welfare of the Boston Public Schools allows us to prioritize a neglected portion of Jesus' mandate to the church. Jesus said this in Acts 1:8, ". . . and you will be my witnesses in Jerusalem, and in all Judea and Samaria, and to the ends of the earth." Jerusalem was the first major city where Christians were called to bear witness. That didn't mean that once they had told their stories of faith and transformation that the work in the city was over. Today, while the global outreach of the church continues to focus on taking the gospel to the ends of the earth, there is still much work that needs to be done in major cities like Boston. It is easy for people who live in suburbs outside of the city to enjoy its sports teams, parks and business opportunities, while forgetting the on-going needs of urban communities. Our partnership efforts in the Boston Public Schools allow us to have a way to make ministry in the big city simple and personal. We like to think we are making a difference in the city for Christ, one student at a time. In doing this, we are re-discovering the city-first part of Jesus' mandate.

4. Serving in this partnership engages us in a dream that is bigger than ourselves. Through a handful of opportunities to tell the story of our two churches, we have become part of a shared dream of linking every church in the Boston area with at least one evangelical church or with an urban-suburban church partnership. One of the questions we are grappling with centers on whether or not we can share and impart a vision that leads other evangelical churches to re-discover the city-first aspect of that mandate. My belief is that Jesus was dropping a clue for future generations about the link between major cities and sustained evangelistic outreach.

5. Serving in this partnership provides a vehicle for participating locally in biblical justice concerns. Some people recoil when I use the term "biblical social justice" because adding the word social can link this to political concerns or ideology. Yet the Bible calls God-fearing people to work for justice in both the Old and New Testaments. The minor prophets in particular called out communities for failing to care for their neighbors or even the country next door. Jesus summed all of that up when he told us to love our neighbors as ourselves. Who are our neighbors? People in the suburbs might be tempted to say that

our neighbors are simply those who live next door, those who look like us and share the same local concerns. Yet Jesus pushed us to think farther than that when he answered the question, "And who is my neighbor?" His story of the Good Samaritan forces us to realize that our neighbor is often a person from the next city or province, who happens to either show kindness or need kindness from us. By all means, let's send Christ-followers to the ends of the earth. At the same time, let's remember the neighbor-first part of Jesus' mandate to the church.[17]

Similarly, at the Trotter Innovation School, Global Ministries Christian Church (a historically black church in Boston) and Grace Chapel (a multiethnic, multisite church in Boston's suburbs) have had a long-standing friendship over many years. They have engaged in service projects, teacher appreciation events, volunteering with the food pantry, mentoring, and supporting the parent council's activities. Pastor Bryan Wilkerson, senior pastor at Grace Chapel, shared these lessons for his church:

1. We're here because we believe that education opens the door to a more promising future. We know this to be the case in developing nations all over the world. As I've had opportunity to travel to such places in recent years, I have seen again and again the sacrifices families will make to get even one of their children a modest education. . . . These families and children recognize that an education can dramatically change the trajectory of that child's life—and the family's life. What's true around the world is true here at home, as well. . . .

2. We're here because we believe that as our cities go, our culture goes. All over the world, people are flocking to cities. Here in the US, immigrants are settling in urban centers. Cities are becoming the financial, commercial, and artistic "nerve centers" for entire regions. What happens in the cities—culturally, intellectually, and spiritually—will shape life and thought in this twenty-first century. Suburban and urban communities must recognize their inter-dependence, and enter into genuine partnership for the welfare of the city.

17. Emmanuel Gospel Center, "How Churches Can Make a Difference in the City of Boston," Learning Communities: Guidebook for Boston Church-School Partnerships, 2014.

3. We're here because we believe that children matter to God. Throughout the Bible, we find children being included in God's plan and purposes. God calls on the community not only to provide for and protect children, but to nurture their minds, hearts, and spirits. As followers of Jesus, we are inspired and challenged by his love for children, and by the value he bestowed on them with his words and his attention. When we work to improve a child's health, happiness, and opportunities in life, we not only bring a smile to their face, but to God's, and ours, as well.[18]

Pastor Bruce Wall, one of the lead pastors at Global Ministries, shared why he chooses to have his church participate in a school partnership with Grace Chapel:

I believe in the Body of Christ. I also believe that urban and suburban Christians need to work together and show forth the true essence of the Body. Also, crossing the racial barrier is very important to me. Grace Chapel and Global Ministries Christian Church have had a rich history of working together in New England, across the country and world-wide in reaching the lost men and women with a message of hope. The schools in Boston have never been as open to working with the churches as they are through these church and school partnerships. Working with Grace is like working with my family.[19]

It has been beautiful to see the ways in which the Body of Christ has been willing to work together with the same goals and purposes in mind, seeing the value in collaboration. If we were to dig deeper, we would find these churches do not share the same theological views on every issue. However, the leaders from these churches share a love for Boston, a vision for mobilizing their congregations to serve a school community, and a desire for their churches to learn from each other, to contribute their unique resources, and to increase their impact by working together.

---

18. Emmanuel Gospel Center, "Why Are We Here?" Learning Communities: Guidebook for Boston Church-School Partnerships, 2014.
19. E-mail from the Reverend Bruce Wall, May 12, 2016.

Often, the needs of the schools can feel overwhelming for one church to take on by itself. The community support that comes from churches collaborating provides a more sustainable model for school partnerships.

The Dream

As an educator, ministry leader, and program director, I see the journey toward educational attainment as the means to finding purpose in life and fulfilling one's God-given potential. It is a means to an end and not an end in itself. Since education is a part of most people's life experiences, whether good or bad, it becomes an opportunity for those who journey alongside students to form trusting relationships with students and perhaps become the catalyst or support they need to pursue their life goals. Those who come alongside students in their life journeys also have opportunities to build relationships with the other adults in these students' lives, whether family members or teachers.

Also, if one were to see education more holistically, then the well-being of the people socially, emotionally, spiritually, physically, and academically all matter. Supporting students in the fullness of their educational experiences is a tremendous opportunity for churches to live out the mandates to love their neighbors, to care about justice, to be salt and light in this world.

One of the keys is relationship. Some churches might build stronger relationships with students while others might build stronger relationships with the adults. The impact that we make could be with anyone that God brings across our path.

Furthermore, while many churches invite the community to participate in educational programs and events at the church, they could be missing an opportunity to serve and engage with people who do not walk through the church doors. One church shared a story about a teacher who, when the churches were first introduced at the school as partners, had asked, "What if we don't believe in your Jesus?" The pastor responded that it was perfectly fine if she did not believe in their Jesus. They were there to serve as an expression of their faith with no strings attached. Later that day, after the churches had a brainstorming session with the teachers and listened to the needs that they saw, the same teacher thanked him for their partnership and support. This is an opportunity for our churches to step into other people's worlds to listen and learn, before earning the right to invite them into ours. It is a different approach than only running programs within our churches.

As a Christian who cares about seeing the gospel lived out and shared, I also care about justice and believe the Church has a role to play in addressing the inequities in our world. Amos 5:24 (ESV) says: "But let justice roll down like waters, and righteousness like an ever-flowing stream." As one of my colleagues recently prayed, we want to see our churches live out their mandate where justice *and* righteousness both go forth equally and there is a balance. I do not see the conflict for churches to seek righteousness, live out the gospel, *and* at the same time seek to address injustices in our communities. These values are not mutually exclusive.

While it might feel easier to do things alone, our churches miss out on so much growth and learning by not partnering with other churches, even those with different theological viewpoints. If churches share the same vision to see all children have an equal opportunity to thrive with access to resources to achieve their goals, they should be able to work together toward that purpose. Sure, there will still be disagreements in theology and differences in culture among churches. However, partnering together around common goals can help our churches build genuine relationships with each other that help tear down the walls that are too prevalent in our world today.

From a distance, churches and Christians all along the racial or theological spectrum can easily "play it safe" by engaging only like-minded churches and leaders, while allowing explicit or implicit stereotypes, prejudices, or judgments of the "other" race, denomination, or church hinder us from seeing each other through God's lens and following in his example of humility and love. As churches rally around common concerns and collaborate, the natural settings provide opportunities to build genuine friendships and trust. Trust deepens as we learn about each other's character and heart even as we learn to work together across our different perspectives and approaches to organization or strategy. I have seen white churches sometimes plan meetings and events very differently from black or Latino churches. However, when they work together, the leaders from these churches learn to submit to one another and to understand each other's style and preference for how to engage their own congregants. Sometimes, these differences make the work happen more slowly or lead to challenges. Over time, though, the churches learn to appreciate each other's strengths and how they can complement each other.

So what is the dream? The dream is to see more churches in greater Boston step outside of their walls to experience the richness of stepping into

other worlds, such as the schools and churches different from theirs. We
want to see the churches rise up to seek the welfare of all children and their
families. If church partners engage at multiple levels with their schools and
value the journey of building relationships with people, they will be able to
experience their own personal transformation as well as the transformation
of others. If churches across geographical and ethnic lines partner together
to serve the same schools, they will be able to taste the fullness of being part
of the Body of Christ and be refined further as they learn to love each other.

Jesus said: "A new commandment I give to you, that you love one another:
just as I have loved you, you also are to love one another. By this all people
will know that you are my disciples, if you have love for one another."[20] What
a witness it would be to the world if the Good News of Christ's love, servant-
hood, and humility were to be embodied by all of our churches in the ways
they serve their school partners and each other so that no one could deny
that they are Christ's followers! There is so much potential for the church to
fully live up to its calling to be the salt and light of the world, and we have an
amazing opportunity to achieve this through loving our school communities.

---

20. John 13:34–35 (ESV).

Epilogue

Lallie B. Lloyd

The man bent over his guitar,
A shearsman of sorts. The day was green

They said, "You have a blue guitar,
You do not play things as they are."

The man replied, "Things as they are
Are changed upon the blue guitar."
                    —Wallace Stevens, "The Man with the Blue Guitar"

My journey into partnerships between churches and schools took a big turn one hot July afternoon in 2009. I was having lunch at an outdoor café on Boylston Street in Boston with the Reverend Anne Bonnyman, then rector of Trinity Church, across the street on Copley Square. I had recently returned from that summer's General Convention of the Episcopal Church in Anaheim, California, and I was telling Anne that I felt some disappointment.

Convention had passed Resolution B025, which urged dioceses to encourage every parish to partner with a public school, Episcopalians to give forty hours a year "in support of public education through direct service, participation in community based educational enrichment opportunities, advocacy and/or teacher support," and called on the federal government to "support policies and funding priorities that support equity in public education for all young people.[21]"

As Bishop Catherine Roskam describes in her chapter in this volume (see chapter 6), this resolution grew out of her awareness that children living in poverty in New York were being denied the quality education they deserved, that a relationship with a mentor or tutor can make a real difference in a child's life, and that community-based enrichment, advocacy, and teacher support can transform school quality.

By the summer of 2009 I was still hoping for more from the Church. I had gone to General Convention looking for directed action, a path forward together, a community of shared purpose, accountability. I wanted the Church's response to reflect more urgency. Let me back up and show you some of where that desire came from.

My Journey

My four siblings and I were raised outside Philadelphia in a white affluent family. My mother was an active volunteer, and my father was an investment banker. They both came from socially prominent families and had the resources and the desire to send my siblings and me to private schools. I went to a Quaker elementary school where I studied the "New Math" (this was 1964) in sixth grade and played outside three times a day; later I went to boarding school in Connecticut, which prepared me for an Ivy League college. I was lucky and I am grateful.

But I was also ignorant.

I thought parents who *really* cared for their children would all send them to "good schools" like the ones I attended. I didn't know how expensive private school was. I didn't know that Haverford, like most suburbs, had been designed by federal lending programs, and redlined by bankers, to exclude black families, or that local zoning regulations restricted high-density housing, thereby excluding many blue-collar and working-class families. I didn't know that while the GI Bill provided college scholarships for veterans of WWII, college admission quotas kept many blacks out of the most rigorous and prestigious colleges, and that the limited enrollment capacity of the

---

21. General Convention, *Journal of the General Convention of . . . The Episcopal Church, Anaheim, 2009* (New York: General Convention, 2009), 710.

colleges black GIs could attend restricted the educational opportunities of an entire generation. I didn't know that the federal guarantee of first-time mortgages for GIs was restricted to whites buying houses in white neighborhoods.

They said, "You have a blue guitar,
You do not play things as they are."

The man replied, "Things as they are
Are changed upon the blue guitar."

I was raised to believe that "things as they are" were right and precisely as they were *meant* to be.

My inherited racialized, self-justifying beliefs about privilege and stereotypes of others went unchallenged for too long. I was isolated and living in a worldview that justified my privilege.[22] The consequences of my isolation were ongoing ignorance and separation from black and brown peers whose friendship and life experiences would have enriched mine.

When I was a child, my family attended the Episcopal Church of the Redeemer in Bryn Mawr on the weekends we were home. When I was seventeen, an awareness grew in me that believing in God should make a difference in how I lived my life. My family's lives looked just like everyone else's I knew, and I sensed God wanted more.

I married when I was nineteen and a few years later, my husband, Scott, and I moved to Guilford, Connecticut, where we worked as resident directors for the Guilford A Better Chance program.[23] Founded in 1963, this national program gives talented students from under-resourced high schools "a better chance" at college success by inviting them to attend a public or private college preparatory high school, with lots of academic and personal support.

Students came to Guilford from urban neighborhoods across the Northeast: the South Bronx, North Philadelphia, Cleveland, and Roxbury. The "girls," as Scott and I referred to them, doubled the black population of Guilford High School, and a few have told me recently that in retrospect they feel like they won the life lottery. It was a great opportunity for them.

22. See Debbie Irving's *Waking up White, and Finding Myself in the Story of Race* (Cambridge, MA: Elephant Room Press, 2014) for a description of her journey from a similar background to becoming a white advocate for racial justice.
23. See http://www.abetterchance.org.

Scott and I lived there for two years while he completed seminary, and we tried to make a home for the students. Every school night I cooked dinner for nine, and we coached their English essays and Algebra 2 problem sets. I came to see the town of Guilford, which looked something like Haverford, through their eyes, and this changed me. It changed my life. It was my blue guitar. It was a great opportunity for me.

We left Guilford in 1978. Scott was ordained an Episcopal priest, and we moved to Philadelphia. We had three children. I went to business school and began a career in nonprofit management with a focus on education. Scott died of an aortic dissection at age forty-two in 1994. Life got very complicated.

An Awakening

Deep in my imagination, in my soul, one question lingered over the years after we left Guilford: What about the students left behind? In the South Bronx, in North Philadelphia? What about the students in Compton? In Ferguson?

What kind of people are we in this country if we rely on students' winning the life lottery to have a better chance at life? What kind of Christians are we if we accept this present reality as the best we can do for one another? Is that the American way? Is that God's dream? I didn't think so.

All this was stirred up in me over lunch with Anne that July day, because I wanted more. Anne is an experienced pastor, and she heard my disappointment. Her eyes got big.

"Lallie," she said, "I have an opportunity for you. Trinity has been invited to participate in a neighborhood coalition to keep the Dearborn School in Roxbury open. I don't have time to participate. Will you represent Trinity Church? Will you bring back to us what you're learning? Will you help that team reach its goal?" Of course I said, "Yes." How could I refuse?

I'd spent the decades since Guilford tracking the data that shows us, for example, that only 73 percent of black ninth graders finish high school on time, compared to 87 percent of white students.[24] And statistics about the devastating impact of poverty on education:

---

24. National Center for Education Statistics, "Data Tables for Common Core of Data," http:// nces.ed.gov/ccd/tables/ACGR_RE_and_characteristics_2013-14.asp (accessed December 2016).

- In 2013, for the first time ever in history, more than half of all public school students lived below the official poverty level ($23,021 for a family of four).[25]
- By the end of the fourth grade, African American and Hispanic students are behind their white counterparts by the equivalent of about two grade levels.[26]
- Dropout rates of sixteen- to twenty-four-years-olds from the lowest quartile of household incomes are three times higher than those from the highest quartile.[27]

But I also knew that we do—actually—know what works. With the right support children can overcome the health, developmental, and learning deficits of poverty. The research and data on what works point toward these principles:

- High quality early childhood education programs
- Reducing class size
- Medical and social services
- Protecting democratic control of public schools
- Reducing racial and income segregation[28]

The problem is that it's expensive.

---

25. Steve Suitts, *A New Majority Research Bulletin: Low Income Students Now a Majority in the Nation's Public Schools* (Atlanta, GA: Southern Education Foundation, 2015), 2. http://www .southerneducation.org/Our-Strategies/Research-and-Publications/New-Majority-Diverse -Majority-Report-Series/A-New-Majority-2015-Update-Low-Income-Students-Now

26. Ulrich Boser, Perpetual Baffour, and Steph Vela, *A Look at the Education Crisis: Tests, Standards, and the Future of American Education* (Washington, DC: Center for American Progress, January 2016), 9. Citing National Center for Education Statistics, "2015 Mathematics and Reading TUDA Assessment Report Card: Summary Data Tables with Additional Detail for Average Scores, Achievement Levels, and Percentiles for Districts and Jurisdictions." https://www.americanprogress.org/issues/education/reports/2016/01/26/129547/a-look-at-the -education-crisis/

27. J. McFarland, P. Stark, and J. Cui, *Trends in High School Dropout and Completion Rates in the United States: 2013* (NCES 2016-117) (Washington, DC: U.S. Department of Education, National Center for Education Statistics, 2016), table 2.1, p. 57. Retrieved December 20, 2016, from http://nces.ed.gov/pubsearch.

28. Diane Ravitch, *Reign of Error: The Hoax of the Privatization Movement and the Danger to America's Public Schools* (New York: Vintage Books, 2014), 225–312.

And all during those in-between years while I was in graduate school, working and raising my children, my soul was restless, asking, "Where is the church? Have we forgotten God's dream of abundance? Have we forgotten our own history?"

I went to Episcopal Divinity School to study our Anglican theology and the Episcopal Church's history of social justice movements, to learn about heroes from the past and meet contemporary ones. That's where I began to see the power dynamics of race, and where "things as they are" became more visible to me.

That's when I realized that in today's culture those of us with social and political power (who are mostly white) don't want to pay for those well-researched, well-staffed, and well-managed programs. This is the truth of "things as they are," though it hurts to take that in.

Ta-Nehisi Coates puts it this way, "[A] society that protects some people through a safety net of schools, government-backed home loans, and ancestral wealth but can only protect you with the club of criminal justice has either failed at enforcing its good intentions or has succeeded at something much darker."[29]

So, yes, I said, "Yes" to Anne's invitation. I joined the Dearborn Community Alliance, a coalition of pastors, parents, teachers, students, and community leaders, all supported by the Greater Boston Interfaith Organization (GBIO). We were Christian, Jew, and Muslim. The Christians were Baptists, Episcopalians, and Presbyterians. We built on fifteen years of GBIO's organizing and relationship building; it took two more years to get approvals from the city of Boston, the Commonwealth of Massachusetts, and the Boston Public Schools.

At a personal level, Yusufi Vali, GBIO's lead organizer for the Dearborn, became my first Muslim friend. One day over coffee he told me how moved he is by the beauty of his community reciting the entire Qur'an together, which they do every year during Ramadan. His story reminded me of the beauty I experience at our Easter vigil, when we tell our entire Christian story of salvation.

I was changed.

And there were three other outcomes of my saying "Yes" to Anne.

---

29. Coates, *Between the World and Me.* 17–18.

First, the Dearborn School, which, had it closed, would have been a cavernous abandoned building in a residential neighborhood. Instead the new Dearborn School is scheduled to open in the fall of 2018, as a grade 6-12 STEM[30] academy, serving students from that same neighborhood.

Second, I led a recruitment drive to get fifty people from Trinity Church into the Dearborn auditorium for a community-wide celebration one Thursday night in March 2012. This connection with the Dearborn helped deepen and enliven Trinity's mission to serve the youth of Boston. Today, under the leadership of another volunteer, more than thirty parishioners work through the Trinity Boston Foundation to tutor students, develop life-changing relationships, and personally connect the congregation to its institutional mission.[31] When I moved out of town, I stopped participating in the Dearborn Community Alliance and Trinity's tutoring program, but what we did together made a difference in both places.

And third: I found my path. In that diverse coalition gathered at the Dearborn, I glimpsed the Kingdom. I saw:

- All the nations—we were working across race, class, and religion;
- And I saw prisoners set free—by access to quality education;
- And I saw the vulnerable—the children of Roxbury—at the center of our attention, right where Jesus tells us they should be. Children are always and everywhere the most vulnerable;
- And I saw joy.

A Forgotten Legacy

Since that night at the Dearborn I've discovered a lot. I learned that universal public education is the church's legacy.

As long ago as 1780 Robert Raikes,[32] a layperson in the Church of England, wanted to do something to reduce the poverty and crime in his city. So he hired a few teachers to teach children to read using the Bible on Sundays, the only day they didn't work in the mills. He also owned a

---

30. Science, technology, engineering, and mathematics.
31. Diana Carson is a Trinity volunteer. You can read her story in chapter 2.
32. See John Carroll Power, *The Rise and Progress of Sunday Schools* (New York: Sheldon & Company, 1833), and C. Stella Davies, ed., *A History of Macclesfield* (Manchester, England: E. J. Morten, 1976), 219–25.

newspaper, and as he publicized what he was doing and how eager the children were to learn, people volunteered to help, and lots of the children came.

Raikes's experiment was the beginning of the Sunday school movement, which we think of as Christian education that happens on Sunday mornings at church in the United States, but his experiment had another much more transforming legacy. Within about fifty years these "Sunday schools" were teaching 1,250,000 children a week. Then, in 1833, and based in part on the evidence provided by these Sunday schools, Parliament made its first grant to build an elementary school at public expense. Since Parliament relied on the data and the evidence provided by the Sunday schools, some have described them as the forerunners of the current English school system.

Why aren't we—as church—talking about this? I wanted to talk about it, so I began calling around looking for other Episcopalians who were partnering with schools.

I found Anita Chan, then a program officer at Trinity Wall Street, who invited me to learn more about the community of church-school partnerships in New York, known as All Our Children—founded by Bishop Catherine Roskam,[33] educators like Joyce Mondesire, and others. Trinity Wall Street invited me to help expand the movement for church-school partnerships nationally.

We held a discernment gathering in Richmond in 2012 with forty people Anita and her colleagues knew. About four from each of ten church-school partnerships from Dallas, Houston, Cleveland, Baltimore, Chapel Hill, New York, and Boston came to Richmond. Our purpose was to build relationships among congregational leaders in active partnerships with urban public schools and discern if there was enough interest to form a network.

For two days we talked and learned together; we shared meals and prayer. We visited the Woodville School, where a partnership with St. Paul's Richmond has been in place for fifteen years.[34] We toured the city of Richmond, learning about its history of racial segregation and current efforts to bring healing to the metropolitan area.

We asked them what they needed. They said they wanted a network to provide relationships, share resources, and change the narrative about public education.

---

33. Read Bishop Roskam's story in chapter 6.
34. Read about St. Paul's and Woodville in chapter 5.

At the end of our time together in November, participants said the most valuable part about our time together included:

- Meeting other Episcopalians who are passionate about public schools
- Having time for reflective conversation about what is meaningful in our work and to focus on our communities and our futures
- Discovering our shared passion
- Seeing the power of prayer and perseverance
- Linking service to social justice
- Finding inspiration and hope in our collaboration
- Hearing honest stories of programs' emergence and growth
- Discovering the variety of projects and their challenges, similarities, and differences
- Seeing programs that were further down the road
- Imagining how we might evolve over time
- Seeing how all the pieces fit together

We asked what they would find most useful going forward, and their answers included:

- Reshaping the narrative about public education in the United States today
- Telling these stories of success—not just publicity, but a different conversation
- Getting the Episcopal Church involved
- Gaining resources for emerging partnerships and new understandings of Christian formation
- Developing Christian formation materials to support faith development for and through community-based justice action

All Our Children

As a result, in 2014 we launched the All Our Children National Network in Baltimore.[35] The network started with twelve members; today it has over ninety members with thousands more connected through our newsletter and social media.

---

35. Hal Ley Hayek, Amy Slaughter Myers, Liz Steinhauser, and Ben Campbell, authors of chapters in this book, were leaders at the Baltimore conference.

All Our Children (AOC) envisions every school having everything every child needs to thrive. Partnering with public schools is an urgent path for people of faith to accomplish this vision. We know partnerships between congregations and schools are an effective path to address racism and economic inequity, serve communities, and revitalize congregations. We are part of a broad national movement to create meaningful improvements in the quality and equity of public education. For congregations with active partnerships we connect leaders and volunteers to form a community of hope, encouragement, and relationships. By fostering this community, creating materials, and hosting events, we shorten the learning curve for those starting the journey.

AOC's mission is to build the movement for education justice by supporting congregations and their members who are exploring, forming, and leading community partnerships with public schools. We seek to energize faith leaders and mobilize congregations by lifting up church-school partnerships' power to bring about racial reconciliation, neighborhood healing, economic equity, and education justice.

In 2015, I asked three bishops, Andrew Waldo[36] of Upper South Carolina, Alan Gates of Massachusetts, and Prince Singh of Rochester to help us develop a resolution for the 78th General Convention of the Episcopal Church. That June, with the additional support of fourteen grassroots church-school partnership leaders from across the country, General Convention endorsed Resolution B005, Endorse Church-School Partnerships to Support Public Education,[37] as a path for following Jesus into the neighborhood, addressing educational inequity, and rejuvenating congregations. The resolution also requested AOC to convene a national symposium on "The Role of the Church in Addressing Educational Inequity," which will be held in early 2018.

Church-School Partnerships Change the World

Church-school partnerships change the world. I believe they do this in three ways: they change lives, they change communities, and, because they change

---

36. Read Andrew Waldo's story in chapter 8.
37. Resolution 2015-B005: Endorse Church-School Partnerships to Support Public Education
http://episcopalarchives.org/cgi-bin/acts/acts_generate_pdf.pl?resolution=2015-B005
(accessed February 15, 2017).

lives and communities, they hold a mirror to our internalized biases that keep "things as they are" in place.

They change lives.

A partnership with a school can change the lives of students through tutors and mentors. Robert Putnam writes, "If America's religious communities were to become seized of the immorality of the opportunity gap [between children of affluence and children of poverty], mentoring is one of the ways in which they could make an immediate impact."[38] Reading buddies and tutors can help children read on grade level, and research shows that those who are not reading proficiently by the end of third grade are four times more likely to leave school without a diploma.[39]

One day Sophia, a fifth grader I was tutoring, said with a shrug of her shoulders that she didn't really care if she got that third green card for misbehavior, which would mean she had to repeat fifth grade. My alarm bells went off. I know that when a child repeats a grade, especially one who is already bored and acting out, her odds of ever graduating go way down, and so do her options for life. I only had one or two more conversations with her, so I took a risk and leaned in. I said, "Sophia, you know right and wrong. You can make good choices for yourself, and getting that third green card would not be good for you." Months later I learned Sophia had not gotten another green card. She'd made the right decisions for herself, and perhaps I had nothing to do with that, but perhaps I did.

And it's not just the student whose life is changed. One of our early partners has as its tagline, "Tutor a child: Change two lives."[40]

Once a volunteer from Trinity Boston overheard the principal berating a child in the hallway while the volunteer sat nearby with her own student. Later, when we gathered for a potluck supper and she told us this story, she was moved to tears. "What can we do?" She wanted to know, "It's just so wrong." And all we could do was listen to her and bear witness to her pain,

---

38. Robert D. Putnam, *Our Kids: The American Dream in Crisis* (New York: Simon & Schuster, 2015), 259.

39. Annie E. Casey Foundation, *Early Warning! Why Reading by the End of Third Grade Matters,* Executive Summary, p. 1, citing the research of Donald Hernandez, See www.aecf .org/resources/early-warning-why-reading-by-the-end-of-third-grade-matters

40. See Augustine Literacy Project, www.augustineproject.org/.

accompany her in her struggle to stay present to her own student, and to remain in partnership with the school. So we prayed for her, for both students, and for the principal.

They change communities.

More than fifteen years ago, St. Paul's Richmond started its partnership with Woodville Elementary. As we have described elsewhere the Micah Initiative, which grew out of that relationship, today supports and coordinates the more than 125 Richmond faith communities who partner with a school in the city's densely populated inner ring, which is mostly black and poor. From those relationships, which were first forged around serving children, one group of Richmond's civic leaders is now organizing and advocating for full funding for the Richmond Public Schools, while another works to develop a regional mass transit system so people in the city can get to jobs in the mostly white suburban ring.

Outside Charlotte, in Concord, North Carolina, Jackie Whitfield, a retired educator, knew her county needed more high quality early childhood education centers, so she suggested her congregation start one. They used the land they already had, the people they already knew, and their shared longing to find the resources they needed to make a huge difference in the lives of children and families.[41]

By changing lives and communities, they hold a mirror to our internalized biases that keep "things as they are" in place.

Around 1990, more than twenty years before my lunch with Anne Bonnyman, I made a site visit to Central Park East Secondary School, founded by the pioneer educator Deborah Meier. Central Park East is in East Harlem, and every student qualifies for free and reduced lunch, an indicator of family poverty. My tour guide was a young adolescent with a warm, direct gaze. As he led me around the school building, he stood straight and told great stories through a winning smile. My biased brain said, as if I heard the words spoken out loud, "He can't be poor."

You see, I could tell from being with him that he was smart—so my unconscious brain had to work *hard* to maintain the falsehoods I had absorbed

---

41. Read Jackie Whitfield's story in chapter 3.

from the social context that raised me. I don't think anyone ever said it to me directly, but they didn't need to. I had absorbed and accepted as truth that black children born in poverty could not be smart. That's why they don't need good schools.

Ouch.

In front of me stood a black student who was smart. So with the dangerous logic of unconscious race bias, I tried to twist things around and persuade myself that he—therefore—could not be poor.

And the Holy Spirit called me on it. By the grace of God—and with Debbie Meier's voice ringing in my ears—I heard how self-serving and how wrong my thinking was.

And this gets me to the heart of why church-school partnerships will change the world: our relationships and direct experience are the only challenges to our unconscious bias that we *might* let in.

Partnerships bring services and relationships that schools need, but that's not their biggest impact. The transformative potential of partnerships is that they change the volunteers. People who mentor a child or volunteer at an under-resourced school, especially people like me from white affluent or middle-class backgrounds, step into relationships and experiences that change how we see the world. In fact, these relationships and experiences are the most powerful and direct way to change attitudes, worldview, perspective, and culture.

It's human nature to ignore evidence that conflicts with the cognitive frames we use to make meaning of our world. We all do it. People—all of us—see and interpret the world through our own personal lenses. We are meaning-making creatures, and we impose meaning on everything we perceive. We overlay patterns based on what we believe to be true, whether or not these patterns fully conform to the evidence before us. These patterns are socialized, usually learned at home and absorbed unconsciously along with the values, habits, and norms of our culture. They are not objective, neutral, or universal. We often mistake our perceptions for reality. In other words, while we see the world subjectively, we often believe our perceptions to be objective, and end up biased without being aware.

So we rarely change our values or attitudes based on argument; most of us choose instead to ignore the facts and evidence. But it's harder to ignore or throw away the impact of our own lived experience—relationships and direct knowledge of people different from ourselves. It is only through our personal experience and relationships, which are embodied, personal, and heart-centered, that our beliefs and attitudes are challenged.

If we put ourselves in unfamiliar places, if we allow atypical experiences to become familiar, if we build relationships across boundaries of race, class, and geography, our own direct experiences can cause us to do a double take. Church-school partnerships give us relationships and experiences that invite us to reexamine our otherwise unexamined bias.

Ingrained biases affect what we project onto people we see as different from us, on those we name as Other. Affluent and middle-class whites are likely to see people of color, people living in poverty, and non-native English speakers as Other. When saturated with the racial prejudice so prevalent in America, inner beliefs and mental models often become implicit race bias. White people need to take responsibility for the presence of implicit bias in ourselves as individuals and in our formal and informal social structures, including schools.

Contemporary crises and conversations provoked by the murder of unarmed black civilians by law enforcement, racial profiling, and the differential in criminal justice treatment and sentencing between accused white and black people demonstrates that race-based prejudice operates at the interpersonal, local, and structural level. Race-based prejudice creates emotional, social, and geographic distance between the perpetrator of the prejudice and the object of that prejudice, and that distance allows the seeds of fear to germinate into hate. White people need to recognize and take responsibility for the fact that the danger inherent in that distance goes only one way. People of color suffer physical, economic, and emotional harm from race prejudice exponentially more than white people do.

How does this connect with partnerships between church volunteers and schools?

When volunteers arrive at the schoolhouse door with race bias, especially when that bias is unconscious, they are opening themselves to experiences and relationships that can challenge their mental models. If they arrive assuming they have answers, believing they are doing the school a favor, and perceiving their culture to be normative, they may be guilty of toxic charity.

On the other hand, those who come with open hearts and open minds, and culturally competent team leaders, may have a Pauline experience of heartbreak, repentance, and scales falling from their eyes.42 Abstractions about poverty and justice become highly personal when they impact the life of a child you have come to love, or a teacher who has invited you into her classroom every week.

Stepping into relationships that will change us is following Jesus's call to incarnational love. By showing up with an open mind and an open heart, we open ourselves to being changed and that may be the biggest gift we can make.

So church-school partnerships—even those that begin as direct service or donation-based relationships—have the potential to transform the attitudes, beliefs, and expectations of people involved in them. Cumulatively, these are the changes that change culture and build social movements.

There are no guarantees that partnerships will have this impact. It's up to the leaders and participants to inform themselves and stay open to people different from themselves, and to learn about internalized bias—both their own and others. But for the church, these partnerships can be a way into one of the most urgent challenges facing our country today, a way to build relationships in our communities and a way to invite the Spirit to make us new.

When volunteers arrive at the schoolhouse door with race bias, especially when that bias is unconscious, they are inviting experiences and relationships that could challenge their mental models. If they arrive assuming they have answers, believing they are doing the school a favor, and perceiving their culture to be normative, they may be guilty of toxic charity.

On the other hand, those who come with open hearts and open minds, and culturally competent team leaders, may have a Pauline experience of heartbreak, repentance, and scales falling from their eyes.[43] Abstractions about poverty and justice become highly personal when they impact the life of a child you have come to love, or a teacher who has invited you into her classroom every week.

Stepping into relationships that will change us is following Jesus's call to incarnational love. By showing up with an open mind and an open heart, we open ourselves to being changed, and that may be the biggest gift we can make.

42. Acts 9:18.
43. Acts 9:18.

So church-school partnerships—even those that begin as direct service or donation-based relationships—have the potential to transform the attitudes, beliefs, and expectations of people involved in them. Cumulatively, these are the changes that make change culture and build social movements.

There are no guarantees that partnerships will have this impact. It's up to the leaders and participants to inform themselves and stay open to people different from themselves, and to learn about internalized bias—both their own and others. But for the church, these partnerships can be a way into one of the most urgent challenges facing our country today, a way to build relationships in our communities and a way to invite the Spirit to make us new.

God's Mission

The people I've met through this work, the places I've gone, and the communities I've visited have changed the way I read the news. They've changed the headlines that jump off the screen, and the questions I have for people running for office. They have changed whom I vote for.

When I reminded Sophie that she knows right from wrong, when we sat and wept together because of emotional violence at a school, when we witnessed the Kingdom in the Dearborn auditorium, we were being changed into the ones God needs here and now to bring about the necessary changes in the way we do education in this country.

The opportunity provided by a partnership between a congregation and a school is to do this work together as Christians—to pray together, and ask questions that are not appropriate at school:

- Where is God in this?
- Where did I see the face of Jesus today?
- What does it mean to be building the Kingdom?
- What is the difference between charity and justice, and why does that matter?

Asking, praying, and living these questions deepens our faith. And when, in community and in prayer, we seek answers to questions like this, God will answer us. And God's answers will change us and change our world.

The church's role in working for education justice is essential and unique, because we are drawn forward by our faith in the goodness of God's ongoing creation, which is meant for all. We used to think the mission of the church was to go to other places and tell other people about God, Jesus, and the church. We're coming to a different understanding now in these opening decades of the twenty-first century. We're figuring out that we had it flipped around.

It's not so much that the church has a mission, but that God has a mission of healing and reconciliation that is already active and abroad in the world. God has a mission in our hearts, our congregations, and our communities.

Those of us called to All Our Children want to serve God's mission of providing excellent education so all our children grow into the fullness for which they were created.

We are the ones who need to do this, even though we're not going to get it right all the time. But our call is to keep showing up, to keep getting it "good enough." We are the ones who are needed. Our open hearts, our hands, our willingness to love, to risk change, and heartbreak is what is needed.

It is our hope and expectation that those partnerships will lead to action: to alliances with other faith communities, education advocates and activists; to organizing campaigns for school libraries, or universal pre-K, or restorative discipline. Whatever next step your community is ready to take. Maybe it's shifting from high-stakes testing to portfolio assessment, maybe it's reducing class size or putting more social workers in each school.

Please join us. Congregations, dioceses, nonprofit organizations, and individuals can join All Our Children. You can contact us, join the movement, and find everything you need on our website: AllOurChildren.org.

There are so many things we can do together, if we build the relationships, get close enough to see with our hearts and serve the needs of the children. That's how church-school partnerships will change the world.

Types of Partnerships

For All Our Children, a partnership is a linked relationship between a named congregation and a named school that is recognized by leaders of both institutions. These partnerships come in many shapes and sizes. Outlined below are the most common types of partnerships we see. Many start with one focus and grow over time to include other dimensions of partnership work.

Donation-Based partnerships provide things like backpacks, supplies, books, software, etc. based on needs identified by teachers and school administrators. Donation-based partnerships can be an easy way to introduce partnership work to your congregation and are a great option for congregations who may not be able to provide many volunteer hours.

After-School or Out-of-School Time partnerships provide services to students of the partner school either on school premises or church premises. These programs can focus on things like tutoring, homework help, sports/physical activity, community gardening, arts programs, etc. Many of these partnerships offer school year and summer programming.

Direct Service partnerships have a regular group of volunteers that work on the school's premises to meet needs identified by school administrators. Examples of work done by direct service volunteers include school cleanup, providing classroom help volunteers, running a library, operating a lunch or food program, etc.

Advocacy partnerships form around issues like school budgets, zoning, redistricting, school choice, testing, and more. Advocacy partnerships consist of a group of volunteers willing to organize and participate in community and government processes. They can operate on a small scale by participating in hyper-local school committee meetings or on the larger city or state level.

Ten Steps to a Successful Church-School Partnership[1]

1. *Be a Storyteller*
   - Ask God to show you some of the ways you have been formed for, and called to, this ministry. Pray, journal, talk to friends. Take notes.
   - Mine your memory for an experience or challenge that brought you to a moment of decision or choice and what happened because of the choice you made. Take notes.
   - Craft a story about that choice and its outcome so your values and purpose shine through.
2. *Approach Parish Leaders*
   - Tell your story, use your notes, invite them to share where it connects with their hearts.
   - Explore their sense of the congregation's capacity and commitment for this ministry.
   - Ask who else in the church or wider community you should talk to.

---

1. You can download this as a handout from www.allourchildren.org/tools/starting-a -partnership/.

3. *Find Allies*
   - Meet with people one-on-one.
   - Look for people who are also called to this ministry and are willing to spend some time because it's meaningful to them.
   - Find four to six people who will join you on this journey.

4. *Gather at Church*
   - Choose a convenient forty-five-minute time block on Sunday morning.
   - Build relationships in the room.
   - With the help of your allies and parish leaders, decide the next action step ahead of time, then ask people to commit to a next step.

5. *Get Educated*
   - Study your local history of desegregation, busing, redlining, etc.
   - Have a book group in your congregation, so you can learn together. See AOC's "Suggested Reading List" for possible ideas.
   - Watch and discuss "Building the Kingdom through Partnerships" (www.allourchildren.org/building-the-kingdom-video/).

6. *Find a School*
   - Where you are welcome,
   - That has a strong leader,
   - And where your congregation's gifts fit their need.

7. *Introduce Yourself*
   - Make an appointment with school leadership. Be flexible and understanding about delays and schedule changes.
   - Lay the groundwork for a foundation of long-term trust. Seek to learn about the school's biggest needs.
   - Decide together if there is mutual interest in exploring a partnership.

8. *Create a Roadmap*
   - Write it out and share it with your congregation and the school.
   - Keep partnership activity small for the first year, focusing on kids, relationships, and being trustworthy.
   - Clarify roles and responsibilities between school and church liaisons.
   - Agree on what "success" will look like.

9. *Invite Others In*
   - Invite the principal to speak at church.

- Connect your congregation with the school: one-time clean-up projects, teacher appreciation lunches, library volunteers; days and evenings.
- Update your church website and bulletin with anecdotes and lots of photos (make sure you have proper permissions).
- Nurture your volunteers' relationships, host regular check-ins and periodic appreciation events.

10. *Show School Spirit*
- Attend public events at your school like budget meetings, school plays, sports games, open houses, and clean-up days.
- Seek and create positive (only) publicity for the school and partnership.
- Be patient, build on success.

Selected Bibliography

Alexander, Michelle. *The New Jim Crow: Mass Incarceration in the Age of Colorblindness.* New York: New Press, 2010.

Bosch, David J. *Transforming Mission: Paradigm Shifts in Theology of Mission.* Maryknoll, NY: Orbis Books, 1991.

Coates, Ta-Nehisi. *Between the World and Me.* New York: Random House, 2015.

Henderson, Anne T., Karen L. Mapp, Vivian R. Johnson, and Don Davies. *Beyond the Bake Sale: The Essential Guide to Family/School Partnerships.* New York: New Press, 2007.

Irving, Debbie. *Waking up White, and Finding Myself in the Story of Race.* Cambridge, MA: Elephant Room Press, 2014.

Kozol, Jonathan. *Savage Inequalities: Children in American Schools.* New York: Harper Perennial, 1992.

———. *The Shame of the Nation: The Restoration of Apartheid Schooling in America.* New York: Crown Publishing, 2005.

Kujawa-Holbrook, Sheryl A., and Fredrica Harris Thompsett. *Born of the Water, Born of the Spirit: Supporting Ministry of the Baptized in a Small Congregation.* Herndon, VA: Alban Institute, 2010.

Lukas, J. Anthony. *Common Ground: A Turbulent Decade in the Lives of Three American Families.* New York: Alfred A. Knopf, Inc., 1985.

Lupton, Robert D. *Toxic Charity: How Churches and Charities Hurt Those They Help (And How to Reverse It).* New York: Harper Collins, 2011.

Mediratta, Kavitha, and Seema Shah. *Community Organizing for Stronger Schools: Strategies and Successes.* Cambridge, MA: Harvard University Press, 2009.

Meeks, Catherine, ed. *Living Into God's Dream: Dismantling Racism in America*. New York: Church Publishing, 2016.

Newton, Connie, and Fran Early. *Doing Good . . . Says Who? Stories from Volunteers, Nonprofits, Donors, and Those They Want to Help*. Minneapolis: Two Harbors Press, 2015.

Oakes, Jeannie, and John Rogers. *Learning Power: Organizing for Education and Justice*. New York: Teachers College Press, 2005.

Putnam, Robert D. *Our Kids: The American Dream in Crisis*. New York: Simon & Schuster, 2015.

Ravitch, Diane. *Reign of Error: The Hoax of the Privatization Movement and the Danger to America's Public Schools*. New York: Vintage Books, 2014.

Salvatierra, Alexia, and Peter Heltzel. *Faith-Rooted Organizing: Mobilizing the Church in Service to the World*. Downers Grove, IL: InterVarsity Press, 2014.

Smith, Luther E. "Living Into God's Dream of Community." In *Living Into God's Dream: Dismantling Racism in America,* ed. Catherine Meeks, 1–14. New York: Church Publishing, 2016.

Warren, Mark R. "Transforming Public Education: The Need for an Educational Justice Movement." *New England Journal of Public Policy* 26, Issue 1, Article 11 (2014):

Warren, Mark R., Karen L. Mapp, and Community Organizing and School Reform Project. *A Match on Dry Grass: Community Organizing as a Catalyst for School Reform*. New York: Oxford University Press, 2011.

About the Authors

Benjamin P. Campbell is a Pastoral Associate at Richmond Hill and St. Paul's Episcopal Church in Richmond, Virginia. For decades Ben has been a champion of racial reconciliation, social justice, and ecumenical activities in Richmond. He is a member of the Richmond Public Schools Educational Foundation, a founder of the Micah Association, and a board member of the Armstrong Priorities Freshman Academy.

Diana Carson is Co-Leader and Volunteer Coordinator for Trinity Boston Foundation's team at McCormack Middle School's library. She has taught E.S.L. and German on the middle school, high school, and college levels, worked as a writer and producer of education-related content for the web, and consulted for non-profits on web strategy. At church she has been involved in children's and youth ministries for almost twenty-five years.

R. William Franklin was consecrated as bishop of the Diocese of Western New York in 2011. Earlier he was Dean of Berkeley Divinity School at Yale and professor at General Theological Seminary and at St. John's University in Minnesota in the field of Church History and World Mission. Raised in Brookhaven, Mississippi, he grew up amidst the tumultuous Civil Rights Era, witnessing both injustice and prejudice.

Hal Ley Hayek has from the earliest age experienced what education can do to open life's curiosities and joys. His great aunt Louise—whose career began as a teacher in a one-room school in northeastern Iowa—taught him that everyone was able to learn and everyone deserved that support.

Through years in parish ministry Hayek is convinced the future for teaching Christian spirituality requires us to be engaged in the issues of daily life in our neighborhoods.

Audrey Henderson was shortlisted for the 2015 Saltire Society First Book Award and was a 2014 Hawthornden Fellow. Her collection *Airstream* was a finalist for the 2014 Homebound Publications Poetry Prize. Her poems have appeared in *Magma*, *The Midwest Quarterly,* and *Tar River Poetry*. She was a finalist in the *Indiana Review* 1/2 K Award and won second place in the *River Styx* International Poetry Contest.

A. Robert Hirschfeld is the tenth bishop of the Episcopal Church in New Hampshire, consecrated in 2012. For high school he attended Choate Rosemary Hall in Wallingford, Connecticut, graduated in 1983 from Dartmouth College, and completed a Master of Divinity degree at Berkeley Divinity School, Yale University in New Haven. He currently serves as President *ex-officio* on the Board of Trustees for Holderness School and The White Mountain School, both founded by the Diocese of New Hampshire.

Alexizendria Link is a full-time classroom educator working with urban youth and serves as a state delegate to the Massachusetts Teachers Association. A 2014 Black Theology and Leadership Fellow at Princeton Theological Seminary, her ministry includes serving as a lay member of the Executive Council for The Episcopal Church, the Social Justice Commission for the Diocese of Western Massachusetts, Province One's Cultural Competency Task Force, and as a vestry member for St. Luke's Episcopal Church in Worcester, Massachusetts.

Lallie B. Lloyd is a lay leader in The Episcopal Church, a former General Convention deputy, and has served on policy and ministry commissions at the local, diocesan, and wider church levels. In 2012 she co-founded the All Our Children National Network of faith-based community partnerships with under-resourced public schools in order to renew Episcopalians' commitment to education justice. She currently serves as its Executive Director.

Amy Slaughter Myers is the daughter, granddaughter, niece, and cousin of public school teachers, and has long been committed to equity in public education and to insuring that all children have access to excellent public schools. She is currently Associate Rector for Mission and Outreach at Epiphany Episcopal Church in Baltimore, which offers Homework Club, one of the only free before and after school enrichment programs in Baltimore County.

Catherine Roskam served as Bishop Suffragan in the Diocese of New York for sixteen years before retiring to Los Angeles in January of 2012 where she serves as Bishop-in-Charge of St. James-in-the-City in Los Angeles. She is known for her work in congregational development and education, founding the Global Women's Fund of the Diocese of New York, All Our Children Network, and Carpenter's Kids.

Liz Steinhauser is the Senior Director of Youth Programs at St. Stephen's Episcopal Church in Boston. She has over thirty years of professional training and experience as a youth worker and community organizer, especially with youth-led non-profits and labor unions, having been trained by Dr. Marshall Ganz of the Harvard Kennedy School of Government and the Industrial Areas Foundation.

W. Andrew Waldo is the eighth Bishop of the Diocese of Upper South Carolina and known for his leadership as part of the South Carolina Bishops' Public Education Initiative, which seeks to enroll thousands of faithful Christians across denominations as tutors and mentors in South Carolina public schools. He serves locally on the Citizen Advisory Committee of the Columbia Police Department and is a member of Bishops United Against Gun Violence.

Ruth Wong directs the Boston Education Collaborative at Emmanuel Gospel Center in Boston, Massachusetts to support, convene, and mobilize churches and leaders as they seek to empower underserved urban students with the education they need for transformation—in their lives and in their communities. She is passionate about creating learning communities for churches and leaders across racial, socio-economic, and denominational lines.

Jackie Whitfield of Concord, North Carolina is a retired teacher, principal, and director for elementary education for the Cabarrus County Schools as well as an instructional coach for the North Carolina New Schools Project, a life-long Episcopalian, and child advocate. She is Founder and President of the All Saints' Early Childhood Foundation and the 2015 recipient of the Anne Lukaitais Champion for Children Award.